A Different Way of Seeing

*Youth with Visual Impairments
and Blindness*

YOUTH WITH SPECIAL NEEDS

A House Between Homes
Youth in the Foster Care System

A Different Way of Seeing
Youth with Visual Impairments and Blindness

The Ocean Inside
Youth Who Are Deaf and Hard of Hearing

My Name Is Not Slow
Youth with Mental Retardation

Chained
Youth with Chronic Illness

Runaway Train
Youth with Emotional Disturbance

Stuck on Fast Forward
Youth with Attention-Deficit/Hyperactivity Disorder

Why Can't I Learn Like Everyone Else?
Youth with Learning Disabilities

Finding My Voice
Youth with Speech Impairment

Somebody Hear Me Crying
Youth in Protective Services

Guaranteed Rights
The Legislation That Protects Youth with Special Needs

The Journey Toward Recovery
Youth with Brain Injury

Breaking Down Barriers
Youth with Physical Challenges

On the Edge of Disaster
Youth in the Juvenile Court System

The Hidden Child
Youth with Autism

A Different Way of Seeing

Youth with Visual Impairments and Blindness

BY PATRICIA SOUDER

MASON CREST PUBLISHERS

Mason Crest Publishers Inc.
370 Reed Road, Broomall, Pennsylvania 19008
(866) MCP-BOOK (toll free)
www.masoncrest.com

First edition, 2004
13 12 11 10 09 08 07 06 05   10 9 8 7 6 5 4 3 2

Library of Congress Cataloging-in-Publication Data
Souder, Patti.
A different way of seeing: youth with visual impairments or blindness / by Patti Souder.
v. cm.—(Youth with special needs)
Includes bibliographical references and index.
Contents: What's the matter?: you blind?—Humpty Dumpty eyes—I just want things to
be normal again—A jigsaw puzzle with some pieces missing—The sea monster—You're
gonna make it, Lightning Bug—New Horizons camp.
ISBN 1-59084-733-4
ISBN 1-59084-727-X (Series)
1.Children with visual disabilities—Juvenile literature. 2. Children, Blind—Juvenile literature. 3. Blindness—Juvenile literature. 4. Eye-wounds and injuries—Juvenile literature.
[1. Blind. 2. People with visual disabilities.] [I. Title. II. Series.]
HV1596.3.S68 2004
3624'1'0835-dc22   2003018637

Design by Harding House Publishing Service.
Composition by Bytheway Publishing Services, Inc., Binghamton, New York.
Cover art by Keith Rosko.
Cover design by Benjamin Stewart.
Produced by Harding House Publishing Service, Vestal, New York.
Printed in the Hashemite Kingdom of Jordan.

Picture credits:
Benjamin Stewart: pp. 16, 33, 54, 59, 60, 62, 63, 74, 85, 86, 98, 113, 114; Corbis:
pp. 27, 41; Image Source: pp. 28, 31, 116; M. Richard Hearing: pp. 72, 89; PhotoDisc:
pp. 17, 18, 29, 99; Research Foundation/Camp Abilities: pp. 42, 44, 73, 75, 76, 77, 107,
108, 109, 110, 111, 112; Seeing Eye: pp. 101, 102, 103, 104, 115, 117.

CONTENTS

A child with special needs is not defined by his disability.
It is just one part of who he is.

INTRODUCTION

Each child is unique and wonderful. And some children have differences we call special needs. Special needs can mean many things. Sometimes children will learn differently, or hear with an aid, or read with Braille. A young person may have a hard time communicating or paying attention. A child can be born with a special need, or acquire it by an accident or through a health condition. Sometimes a child will be developing in a typical manner and then become delayed in that development. But whatever problems a child may have with her learning, emotions, behavior, or physical body, she is always a person first. She is not defined by her disability; instead, the disability is just one part of who she is.

Inclusion means that young people with and without special needs are together in the same settings. They learn together in school; they play together in their communities; they all have the same opportunities to belong. Children learn so much from each other. A child with a hearing impairment, for example, can teach another child a new way to communicate using sign language. Someone else who has a physical disability affecting his legs can show his friends how to play wheelchair basketball. Children with and without special needs can teach each other how to appreciate and celebrate their differences. They can also help each other discover how people are more alike than they are different. Understanding and appreciating how we all have similar needs helps us learn empathy and sensitivity.

In this series, you will read about young people with special needs from the unique perspectives of children and adolescents who

7

are experiencing the disability firsthand. Of course, not all children with a particular disability are the same as the characters in the stories. But the stories demonstrate at an emotional level how a special need impacts a child, his family, and his friends. The factual material in each chapter will expand your horizons by adding to your knowledge about a particular disability. The series as a whole will help you understand differences better and appreciate how they make us all stronger and better.

—*Cindy Croft*
Educational Consultant

YOUTH WITH SPECIAL NEEDS provides a unique forum for demystifying a wide variety of childhood medical and developmental disabilities. Written to captivate an adolescent audience, the books bring to life the challenges and triumphs experienced by children with common chronic conditions such as hearing loss, mental retardation, physical differences, and speech difficulties. The topics are addressed frankly through a blend of fiction and fact. Students and teachers alike can move beyond the information provided by accessing the resources offered at the end of each text.

This series is particularly important today as the number of children with special needs is on the rise. Over the last two decades, advances in pediatric medical techniques have allowed children who have chronic illnesses and disabilities to live longer, more functional lives. As a result, these children represent an increasingly visible part of North American population in all aspects of daily life. Students are exposed to peers with special needs in their classrooms, through extracurricular activities, and in the community. Often, young people have misperceptions and unanswered questions about a child's disabilities—and more important, his or her *abilities*. Many times, there is no vehicle for talking about these complex issues in a comfortable manner.

This series provides basic information that will leave readers with a deeper understanding of each condition, along with an awareness of some of the associated emotional impacts on affected children, their families, and their peers. It will also encourage further conversation about these issues. Most important, the series promotes a greater comfort for its readers as they live, play, and work side by side with these individuals who have medical and developmental differences—youth with special needs.

—Dr. Lisa Albers, Dr. Carolyn Bridgemohan, Dr. Laurie Glader
Medical Consultants

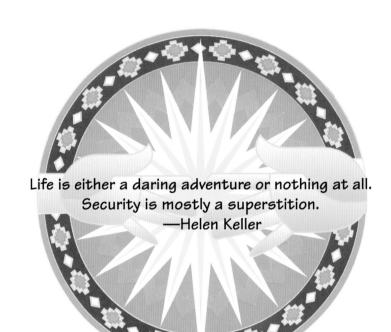

Life is either a daring adventure or nothing at all.
Security is mostly a superstition.
—Helen Keller

1

WHAT'S THE MATTER? YOU BLIND?

Kyla O'Neill squinted up at the scoreboard as she ran down court. *Can't read it!* she thought, catching a bounce pass and going for an easy layup. The ball never even hit the backboard. *What's wrong with me tonight?* Kyla wondered as Maple Grove fans groaned and Lakeview fans chorused, "Air ball!"

Kyla felt her face get warm. *Settle down. Just get the ball back,* she told herself. Kyla focused her attention on Darcy Deevers, Lakeview's point guard. When Darcy tried to pass the ball to her teammate, Kyla managed to get a piece of it. Unfortunately, she also hit Darcy's arm. The ref called a foul.

Darcy's first shot hit the back of the rim and circled inside a few times, eventually dropping through the net to tie the score. Her second shot missed, but Lakeview grabbed the rebound and scored, putting them ahead by two points. Their fans went ballistic.

Arms flailed as Kyla attempted to throw the ball back into play. She searched desperately for a teammate who was free. *Get the ball in bounds or you'll be called for time!* she warned herself, grateful when Megan called, "Ky, over here!"

Where Megan had come from Kyla could only guess. She threw the ball to Megan, then raced to rejoin her team. In the process, she lost track of the ball, seeing it only a millisecond before it smashed into her left cheek. Kyla winced and sucked in her breath.

A heckler yelled, "What's the matter, Carrot-top? You blind?"

"Guess so!" Kyla muttered to herself as the ref called, "Time out! Injury!"

Kyla felt a throbbing pain on the left side of her face. It was minor, however, compared to the embarrassment and sense of failure that crushed her. "You okay?" a medic asked as he guided Kyla off the floor.

"How could I be?" Kyla snapped. "I really blew it. Missed my shots, let Lakeview take the lead, and got hit by the ball." Kyla bit her lower lip to hold back tears. "And I hate being called Carrot-top!"

The medic nodded. "Tough night. We all have them." He stuck out his hand. "My name's Sam. I'm a paramedic. May I get a look at that cheek?"

Kyla nodded. Sam flashed a light over her face and into her eyes. "You wear contacts?" he asked.

Kyla nodded again. "Hey, maybe that's the problem. Maybe my contacts are dirty."

"You having trouble seeing?" Sam asked.

"Some things."

"Just since the collision . . . or before?"

Kyla thought a minute. "I guess things have been kinda fuzzy all night." Kyla closed her left eye gingerly. "Hey, that's better!"

Sam asked her to close her right eye and open her left. "How's that?" he asked.

"Not good," Kyla answered. "Not good at all."

"What do you see?"

"Bright, flashing lights. Some black specks. And a dark cloud right where you should be."

"In that case, you win some eye shields and a trip to the local emergency room." Sam helped her onto a stretcher. He turned to Kyla's parents who had walked over from the bleachers. "You can follow us there."

Kyla wriggled her fingers far enough to feel the ridges on the safety strap and the smooth metal bars that held her in place. She couldn't move her head because it was wedged in some kind of block. She stared up at the ambulance ceiling and wondered what would come next.

Kyla was wheeled into a room with bright lights overhead. A voice to her right said, "Hi, I'm Judy. I'm a nurse and I'm going to check your vital signs."

Kyla heard Sam tell a woman at the foot of the bed, "She was hit pretty hard. Said she saw flashing lights."

So this is what it's like to be blind, Carrot-top.

"How are you, honey?" her mom asked.

"Fine." Kyla tried to ignore the pain in her cheek. "Just wish I could see. I feel like I'm in a beehive where I can hear the bees buzzing but can't see what they're doing."

"Really?" her mother asked. "You can't see at all?"

"Not with these stupid metal cages over my eyes!" Kyla said.

"Oh, of course not." Her mother patted Kyla's arm. "I'm sure you'll be fine. Did the doctor see you yet?"

Kyla was about to say no when the woman who had been talking to Sam said, "Mrs. O'Neill? I'm Dr. Sayer. Sam told me what happened. Now I need to examine your daughter."

Kyla felt a gentle hand on her shoulder as Dr. Sayer asked, "Kyla, how bad's your pain?"

"Not bad," Kyla said.

"It looks like a pretty nasty bruise," Dr. Sayer said. "You sure it doesn't hurt?"

"Well, I guess it does hurt . . . quite a bit, actually," Kyla admitted.

Dr. Sayer told Judy to get an injection, dimmed the lights, and peeled off Kyla's eye shields. After covering Kyla's right eye, Dr. Sayer asked, "What do you see?"

Kyla sighed. "Not much. It's mostly dark with some flickering lights."

Dr. Sayer instructed Kyla to read some eye charts, shined lights in her eyes, and asked questions: When did the flashing lights start? When did the cloudiness begin? Had she been able to see the basket, the scoreboard, and the other players in the game?

Judy poked her with a needle, saying it would "relieve the pain."

Kyla's father came in muttering, "Paperwork!"

"It looks like Kyla has a **_retinal detachment_**," Dr. Sayer finally announced. That's a medical emergency. I'd like to helicopter her to a specialist in Central City right away,"

"Does that mean I'll be blind?" Kyla asked, the blurred feeling around her beginning to disappear as the pain medicine kicked in.

Dr. Sayer took the time to answer Kyla's questions. She explained to her what the words "retinal detachment" meant. And then she said, "The sooner you have surgery, the better your chances are for a good outcome."

WHAT DOES A NORMAL EYE LOOK LIKE?

- The *sclera*, often called the white of the eye, is a firm, fibrous coating that shapes the eyeball and protects the delicate structures within it.
- The *cornea*, sometimes called the window of the eye, is a tough, transparent membrane that covers the front of the eye. It receives and **refracts** light rays and helps the eye focus.
- The *iris* is the colored part of the eye between the cornea and the lens. Its many shades of blue, green, amber, or brown become one of the first things people notice about each other.
- The *pupil* is the round black hole in the center of the iris. Its size automatically changes to regulate how much light enters the eye.
- The *lens* focuses the light rays coming through the pupil to form images on the retina.
- The *retina* is made up of layers of cells that receive light and images and turn them into electrical impulses that are sent to the brain. One layer contains rods and cones. Rods are long rod-shaped cells that respond to light. They provide side vision and night vision. Cones are cone-shaped cells that respond to light, detail, and color. Rods outnumber cones twenty to one.
- The *macula* is the area of the retina that provides the sharp, clear, right-in-front-of-you vision needed for reading, driving, recognizing faces, and seeing fine details. It is one hundred times more sensitive to detail than the rest of the retina because it contains the cones. The fovea, a small depression in the center of the macula, is the place where visual perception is the most acute because it is made entirely of cones.

- The *optic nerve* carries electrical impulses from the macula and retina to the brain where the messages are interpreted into sight.

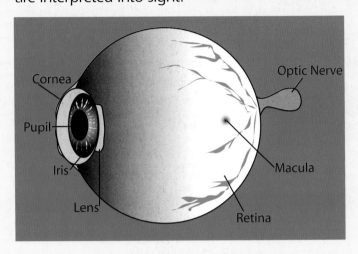

HOW YOUR EYES SEE

Eyes are made up of an incredible number of cells that perform amazing duties to allow us to see near and far at the same time.

Here's how it works:

- Rays of light enter through the cornea, the pupil, and then the lens.
- Internal eye muscles adjust the shape of the lens so it focuses the light rays on the back of the retina.
- Retinal rod and cone cells convert the light into electrical impulses.
- The optic nerve carries the electrical impulses to the brain.
- The brain interprets the electrical impulses by coordinating and merging the images from each eye to produce three-dimensional vision.

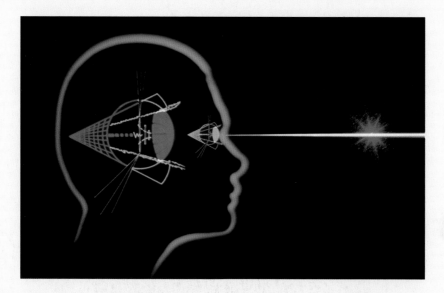

Many people experience problems with the way light is re-fracted from the cornea and lens to the retina. These conditions are called refraction problems and are corrected with glasses or contact lenses.

- *Myopia* (nearsightedness) causes images in the distance to look blurry. This happens because the eye is too long from front to back, causing light rays to meet in front of the retina rather than on it.
- *Hyperopia* (farsightedness) causes eyestrain and blurred vision at close distances. This happens because the eye is too short from front to back and light rays don't focus on the retina as soon as they should.
- *Astigmatism* causes blurred vision, especially of vertical, horizontal, or diagonal lines. It is caused by uneven curves in the cornea.
- *Presbyopia* causes a decreased ability to focus on objects at close range. It occurs when the lenses of

the eyes become harder and less elastic, usually as a result of the aging process.

WHAT'S GOING ON WHEN I SEE STARS OR SPOTS?

Most people see floating black spots (floaters) or flashes of light once in a while because of harmless changes in the **vitreous** and the retina. Sometimes people also see stars when they bump their heads, feel a bad headache coming on, or look at a clear, blue sky.

At other times, floaters and flashes serve as the early warning signs of serious problems such as:

- retinal tears
- retinal detachments
- infection
- inflammation
- hemorrhage

Quick action is needed! Contact your eye doctor immediately if you notice:

- a sudden decrease in vision accompanied by flashes and floaters
- a veil or curtain that cuts off part or all of the vision
- a sudden increase in the number of floaters

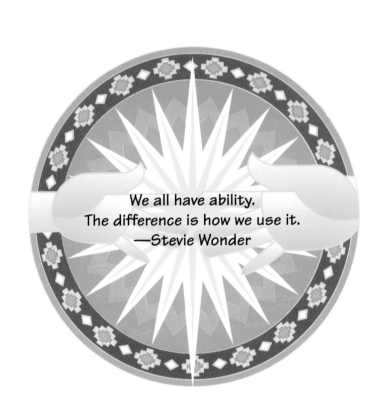

We all have ability.
The difference is how we use it.
—Stevie Wonder

2

HUMPTY-DUMPTY EYES

"Hi, Kyla, I'm Dr. Goodwin, a retinal specialist," a deep voice said. Dr. Goodwin helped Kyla move from the stretcher to a special chair surrounded by long-armed, bespectacled equipment. "I hear a basketball came out of nowhere and whacked you in the face."

Kyla nodded. "Exactly."

"Well, I'm the guy who has to see if you or the basketball won . . . and then try to put you back together again."

"I hope you do better than all the king's horses and all the king's men," Kyla said in a sing-songy way to mimic the nursery rhyme.

"Meaning you're Humpty-Dumpty?"

"Meaning I want to be put back together again—*unlike* Humpty-Dumpty," Kyla said firmly.

"So how about we start by taking off these blinders?"

"Thanks," Kyla said, sure the doctor was tall, dark, and handsome like his voice.

"So what do you think?" he asked, almost as if reading her mind.

Kyla closed her bad eye and said, "You're gray! And kinda short."

"Now what kind of thing is that to tell the doctor who's about to fix your eyes?" Dr. Goodwin winked at her. "I'm younger on the inside than I look on the outside." He looked at his watch. "Why, if I were as old as you think I am, I'd be home in bed." He examined her

21

eyes with a bright light. "Well, that's interesting. Have you been playing with sparklers?"

"Not since the Fourth of July," Kyla answered. "Why?"

"Looks like some sparklers in there to me. How's it look to you?"

"Shooting stars. Fireflies. But I guess you could call them sparklers, too. Actually, it's mostly dark now."

"Okay, let's see if you can read these secret messages." He moved to the other side of the room and pointed.

Kyla squinted at the screen. She read some of the charts with her right eye, but her left eye flunked.

Dr. Goodwin rolled his chair over to her right side and held up a large poster where she could see it.

"Look, Kyla, I've been joking around with you, but you have a pretty serious condition called a retinal detachment." He pointed to the picture on the poster. "The retina is a thin membrane at the back of your eye that helps you see the light and images that come through the cornea and lens. Your retina is being torn away from the layer of blood vessels that feeds it. I'm going to try to reattach it. Otherwise, the tear will just keep getting bigger and you won't be able to see. So what do you think? Are you willing to let me do that?"

Kyla nodded.

"I talked to your parents while you were being delivered by the **chopper stork**. They said we could go ahead if it was necessary. I've already called the surgical team. Any questions before we start?"

"Will it hurt?"

"Some. But we'll give you anesthesia while we do the surgery, and as much pain medicine as you need afterward."

"Okay," Kyla said. "Let's put Humpty-Dumpty together again."

Dr. Goodwin raised his hand for a high five and Kyla slapped it as she was taken to the surgical suite.

When Kyla woke the next morning, she was on her left side. Her mother was squeezing her hand and asking, "Kyla, honey, how are you?"

"I think I'm fine. Hard to tell when you first wake up, though." Kyla yawned, stared at pale blue walls and vertical blinds, and tried to figure out where she was. She reached up and felt a plastic bubble over her left eye. "Hey! Who won the game? And how'd you get here?" she asked as she began to remember the night before.

"I don't know who won the game. We were too busy trying to catch up to your helicopter."

"You mean Dad came, too?"

"Of course. I sent him out to find some breakfast so his stomach wouldn't wake you up." Her mother kissed Kyla on her right cheek. "Now tell me all about your ride . . . and the surgery."

"I can't. I slept through both. Dr. Goodwin made me laugh, though—before torturing me with glaring lights and nasty tests. Then he gave me something and that's all I remember."

A young woman deposited a tray on Kyla's bedside table and hurried down the hall. "Good thing I came," her mother said. "You're not supposed to move your head right now."

"Why not?" Kyla asked.

"Because you've got a gas bubble in there," Dr. Goodwin said, pointing to Kyla's head as he led a parade of medical students into her room.

"Does that mean I'm a Humpty-Dumpty who couldn't be put back together again?"

"No, ma'am," Dr. Goodwin said. "But you do have quite a shiner."

"Do I look real bad?"

"No, you don't, my little Lightning Bug!" Kyla's father said, entering the room with a bag of bagels.

"Oh, Daddy, you always think I look okay," Kyla said as her dad plunked a kiss on her forehead.

Dr. Goodwin introduced himself and his associates.

"How did the surgery go?" Kyla's father asked.

"I had to do some special procedures because the tear was a bad one that involved the ***macula***."

"What's a macula?" Kyla asked.

Dr. Goodwin held up a flip chart with a picture like the one he'd shown her the night before and pointed to a small dot in the center of the retina. "'Macula' comes from the Latin word for spot. The macula is small . . . about the size of a ladybug. But it's important because it allows you to see what's in front of you. And it's the chief player in letting you see things clearly."

"So now I'll have eagle eyes?" Kyla asked.

Dr. Goodwin stepped back and cleared his throat. "I wish I could promise you that," he said soberly.

Kyla flinched at the look on his face.

"Your problem's a little more complex than anyone knew. I reattached your retina. It will take a few weeks, but you should heal fine from the surgery," Dr. Goodwin said.

"So what's the problem?" Kyla's father asked.

"Well, Kyla has two other eye problems." Dr. Goodwin paused to clear his throat. "First, she has a very high degree of ***myopia***, a condition often called nearsightedness."

Kyla's mother cut in. "Kyla's kindergarten teacher discovered that because Kyla couldn't see the letters and numbers the teacher was writing on the board. We took Kyla to the eye doctor right away, and she's been wearing glasses or contacts ever since."

"And needing her prescription increased every year?" Dr. Goodwin asked.

"Sometimes every couple of months," Kyla's mother answered.

Dr. Goodwin nodded. He turned to a new page in his flip chart and pointed to the top eyeball. "The normal eyeball is round, like this one," he said. "Light rays come through the lens and cornea and meet on the retina, providing clear, well-focused vision." He lifted his finger and pointed to the second eyeball. "If you look closely, you can see that this eyeball is longer, more oval, something like a fat egg. When the light rays enter, they come together before they reach the retina. That makes things that are far away look blurry.

The egg shape stretches the retina, making it thinner and more likely to tear. Catch a basketball with your face, and you've got a perfect setup for a retinal detachment. Which is what happened to Kyla last night."

"So, I do have Humpty-Dumpty eyes after all!"

"Well, sort of," Dr. Goodwin said.

"And all the king's horses . . . and all the king's men . . ." Kyla chanted.

"Did put your retina together again," Dr. Goodwin finished.

"But I'm still going to be nearsighted?" Kyla asked.

Dr. Goodwin nodded.

"You said there were two problems," Kyla's father said.

"So I did," Dr. Goodwin said slowly. "I think Kyla may also have a condition called ***macular degeneration***. It's usually seen in older people, but once in a while, young people are also affected." He held up his flip chart. "Remember what I told you about the macula?"

"It helps you see what's in front of you and makes things clear," Kyla said. "So what's wrong with mine?"

"Your macula came loose when your retina detached. But I'm also seeing changes in your retina that look like your macula is malfunctioning. That means you may have a form of ***juvenile macular degeneration***—or ***dystrophy***, as I prefer to call it."

"Can't you do something to stop it?" Kyla's mother asked.

"There are things that can help people see better, but there's no cure for the disease. At least, not yet."

"Are you sure Kyla has it?" Kyla's dad asked.

"We'll do special tests to find out."

Kyla felt as if a dark cloud filled the room. "Humpty-Dumpty eyes for sure," she muttered. "And all the king's horses . . ."

"And all the king's men need to work together to find out what's going on and what we can do to help," Dr. Goodwin finished firmly.

"You sure were a lot more fun last night," Kyla said.

EMERGENCY!

A retinal detachment is a medical emergency that requires immediate surgery.

When the retina separates from its blood supply, vision is lost in that area. Surgery is the only effective treatment. If a tear or hole is repaired before the retina pulls apart or if a detachment is treated before the macula comes loose, vision can usually be saved.

About 40 to 50 percent of people with detachments have severe myopia or nearsightedness; 30 to 40 percent of detachments occur after cataract surgery; 10 to 20 percent follow eye trauma. Young people are most likely to have traumatic detachments.

Retinal detachments are often painless . . . but they can lead to blindness.

Be sure to report to your doctor immediately any of the following symptoms:

- flashing lights
- floaters (little black objects that look like they're moving)
- blurred vision
- a shadow or curtain over part of your vision

WHAT ARE THE SYMPTOMS OF MACULAR DEGENERATION?

- blurring of central vision
- difficulty seeing detail—up close and at a distance
- distortion of lines and shapes
- diminished color vision

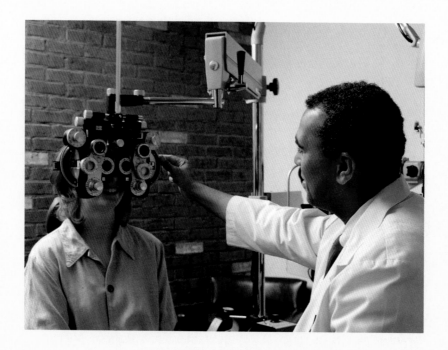

WHAT TESTS HELP DIAGNOSE MACULAR DEGENERATION?

Your doctor will examine your eyes with special lenses to view the interior of the eye through the pupil.
Other tests for macular degeneration include:

- Tests to measure the accuracy of your central vision at specific distances in specific lighting situations.
- Amsler Grid test to check for spots of sight loss.
- Color testing to help determine the status of your cone cells, the retinal cells that interpret color.
- Fluorescein angiogram test to allow your doctor to visualize the inner structure of the eye. Photos are taken of the retina and the macula to identify new blood vessel growth and leakage from blood vessels.

THE AMSLER GRID

One of the tools eye doctors use to help diagnose macular degeneration is the Amsler Grid. People with degenerative diseases can also use it to check their vision at home.

Here's how to use the Amsler Grid:

1. Hold the grid 12–16 inches (305–407mm) from your eyes.
2. Cover one eye.
3. Look directly at the center. If you wear glasses, you should keep them on.
4. Are the lines straight? Or are some of the lines blurred, wavy, or dark?
5. Repeat with the other eye.
6. Call your eye doctor if the lines look blurred, wavy, or dark.

   (Adapted from Macular Degeneration International. An example of the Amsler Grid can be viewed at info@maculardegeneration.org)

Eye doctors use a variety of tests to diagnose various eye conditions.

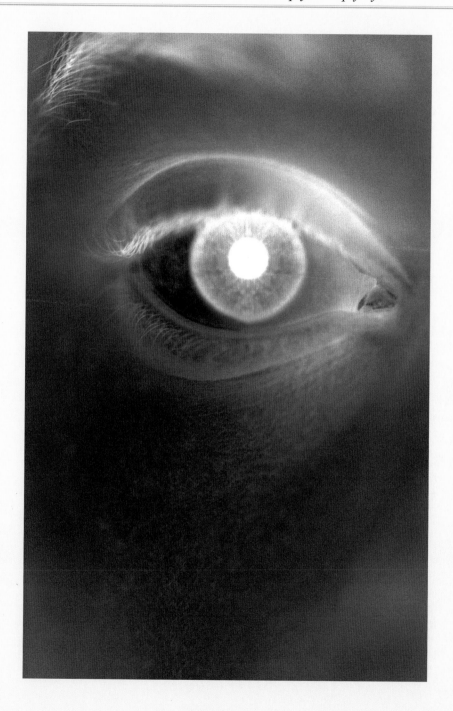

MACULAR DEGENERATION

Age-related macular degeneration (AMD or ARMD) affects 10 million Americans. It's the leading cause of blindness for people over the age of 55. Young people can also be affected by eye disorders involving the macula. Although relatively rare, juvenile forms of macular degeneration cause serious visual impairment for 30 to 50 thousand young people in the United States.

What does this vision thief do?

- It forms a gray or dark cloud that blurs people or objects right in front of the eyes.
- It causes blind spots that make it hard to see details.
- It distorts lines and makes objects look crooked.
- It may cause colors to look faded.
- It makes reading, writing, recognizing people, performing simple tasks like threading a needle, and driving difficult or impossible.

Why does this happen?

- The word "macula" comes from a Latin word meaning spot. It is the name of the ladybug-sized area in the retina, which contains the cone cells that are essential for central and color vision.
- The term "degeneration" refers to deterioration or breakdown.
- "Macular degeneration" refers to several similar conditions characterized by a breakdown of the macula.
- When the macula degenerates, it becomes increasingly difficult to see clearly, especially whatever is in front of the person.
- Macular degeneration is often associated with the

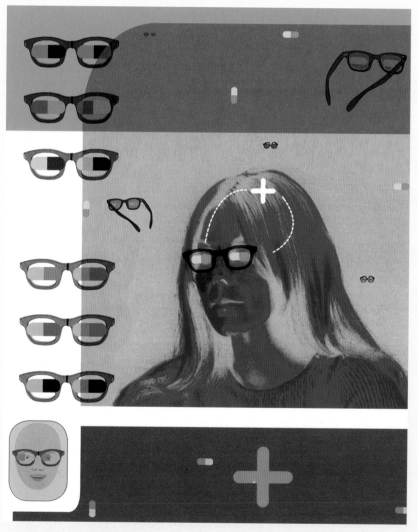

Some visual impairments can be corrected or minimized by wearing glasses.

aging process. Research is being conducted to find the other causes and ways to prevent and treat the condition.

JUVENILE FORMS OF MACULAR DEGENERATION (DYSTROPHY)

Most forms of early-onset macular degeneration are thought to be genetic. The genes needed for normal vision send faulty messages to the cells in the macula. This causes the macula to malfunction and leads to vision loss. Because a malfunctioning macula causes the problem, many re-searchers feel that juvenile forms of macular disease are more accurately identified as macular dystrophies. Stargardt Macular Dystrophy is the most frequent type young people experience. Those with **Stargardt's**:

- usually notice a dark or gray spot in the center of their visual field that blurs whatever is in front of them.
- often complain of having trouble seeing the blackboard and having to hold reading materials closer and closer.
- may be troubled by bright lights or going into a darker place.
- will have trouble recognizing faces and doing simple tasks as their central vision declines.
- may experience a gradual decline in vision from 20/50 to 20/200 or 20/400.

Despite the problems, those with juvenile macular dystro-phies achieve amazing feats. Marla Runyan, the first legally blind athlete to compete in the Olympics, has written a book about her ongoing adjustments with Stargardt's. She says:

To go into the world blind is to play a game of trust. Every day you plunge into a swirl of confusion—and sometimes fear and frustration. The rest of the world has all the information, while you do not. This requires you to strike a delicate and constant balance between wariness and faith. You have a choice: you can get angry, or you can trust in the basic benevolence of the universe and essential goodwill of people, and hope you don't get hurt. Don't we all live that way, really? Blind or not? (From *No Finish Line* by Marla Runyan with Sally Jenkins, published by G. P. Putnam's Sons, 2001)

A student at the Batavia School for the Blind in New York State bends close to read large-print directions for a game during gym class.

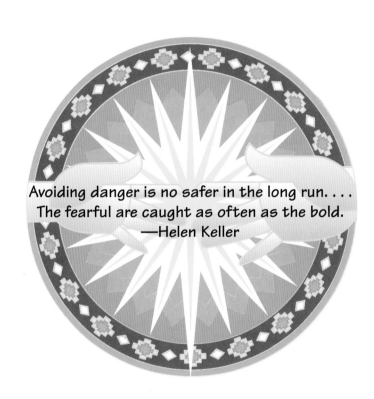

Avoiding danger is no safer in the long run. . . .
The fearful are caught as often as the bold.
—Helen Keller

3

I Just Want Things to Be Normal Again

"You'll need to use eyedrops, wear an eye shield, and keep your head down for three weeks so the bubble presses against the retina correctly and the surgery heals well," Dr. Goodwin told Kyla before she left the hospital late Friday afternoon. "Bend over when you sit or stand. Lie on your left side when you're in bed."

Kyla rode home holding her head in her lap, a balloon bouquet from the basketball team tied to her wrist. As her dad turned onto the gravel road leading to their farm, Kyla braced herself against the bumps while the balloons bounced against the roof. She breathed a sigh of relief when the car finally stopped.

Midnight, their black lab, came bounding to the car. Kyla's dad grabbed his collar and shouted, "Down, Midnight!" as the dog tried to welcome Kyla home by licking her face. Kyla got out of the car and scratched him between the ears.

From her bent-over position, Kyla saw eleven-year-old Abby's legs come running to greet her and then stop. "What's wrong with your back, Kyla?" Abby asked. "I thought you got hit in the face."

Kyla smiled to herself as she pictured the question marks in Abby's big blue eyes. "My back's okay," Kyla told her little sister. "I just have to walk like a hunchback because I have a gas bubble in my left eye."

"Gas in your eye?" Abby asked. "I splashed gas in my eye once and it really hurt! I had to go to the doctor to have it washed out!"

"It's not that kind of gas, Abby." Kyla tried to think how to explain it. "It's kinda like the gas in these balloons."

"Wow! You got a lot of balloons! I wish my friends would send me balloons," Abby said.

Laughing, Kyla stumbled into the steps to the back porch. "Ouch!" she cried, reaching down to rub her shin.

When she looked up, she saw a pair of old dirty sneakers and the bottoms of her brother's jeans coming toward her. Ryan reached out to help her up the steps. "Sorry! I meant to move those steps before you got home."

"Very funny!" Kyla said as something soft rubbed against her feet. "Snowflake!" she exclaimed, reaching down to stroke the soft, longhaired white kitten. Snowflake looked up at Kyla's eye shield and jumped to play with it. "No, Snowflake!" Kyla said, straightening up.

"Kyla!" her mother said, "you have to keep your head down."

"Why does she have to keep her head down?" Ryan asked.

"Because she's got gas in it," Abby answered. "Just like the balloons."

Kyla groaned. "It's going to be a long three weeks."

Kyla had a tough time getting washed and dressed the next morning. When she peeked at herself in the hall mirror, she shrieked, "I look awful! My cheek is black and blue, the shield is ugly, and I look like a gnarly troll. No way is anybody going to see me like this!"

"Hey, sleepyhead!" her dad yelled. "What's taking you so long? I've got a present for you, but I can't wait all day. Ryan and I need to get cracking. It's a great day for making maple syrup."

"Maple syrup!" Kyla shouted. Rushing, she bumped into the doorway. Kyla groaned, rubbing her shoulder. "This stooped-over stuff's old already!"

Kyla held the handrail and walked slowly downstairs. When she got to the kitchen, her dad handed her a wooden tray with a bean-bag bottom.

"Now you can sit up to eat and play games," he said.

"Great!" Kyla said. "What's for breakfast? I'm starving!"

"How about blueberry muffins and milk?" her dad asked. He made a face at her as he bent down to place them on her tray.

"I want to help make maple syrup," Kyla said.

"Not today, Ky," her dad said. "We can't risk having you run into low branches or trip over the tap lines."

"I'll be careful."

"Maybe next time."

Kyla wondered what she'd do the rest of the day, but Abby solved that. "Wanna play Monopoly?"

Inwardly, Kyla groaned. Abby could play Monopoly all day. On the other hand, what else could she do?

An hour later, Kyla thought her back would break. "How about we call it quits, Abby?"

"We can't quit now, Kyla. I just bought Boardwalk and Park Place."

"But everything else you own is mortgaged," Kyla pointed out as she stretched her back to ease the pain.

"Yeah, but when you have Boardwalk and Park Place you can't lose."

Kyla took a deep breath. "Okay, tell you what. I'll give you fifteen minutes to beat me—but only if you sit down here on my level" She pointed to the floor. "My back's killing me, and I'm tired of not being able to see your face."

Abby hunkered down on her knees and they finished the game. Abby ran off shouting, "I won! I won!"

Little sisters! Kyla thought, taking the Monopoly game to the closet. She put it on the top shelf and then realized she'd lifted her head. "Oops!" But she had gotten a glimpse of the blue sky outside, and she felt she had to get out of the house. "Hey, Mom, can I go see Chestnut?" she called.

"*May*, not *can*," her mother corrected. "Although in this case, the real question might actually be *can* as well as *may.*"

"Mom!" Kyla wailed. "I don't need a grammar lesson!"

"But you do need someone to go with you."

"No, I don't!"

"Today you do. I don't want you stumbling over the back steps or crashing into the barn door."

Kyla made a face but kept quiet. Kyla knew she could really mess up her vision if she fell or ran into anything.

Halfway to the barn, Kyla heard Midnight running toward them. "Stop, Midnight!" she shouted, bracing herself for impact.

Her mom grabbed the dog by the collar. "Down, Midnight! Kyla just had surgery." Midnight whimpered a little, then trotted along beside them.

Chestnut whinnied when he saw Kyla, and Kyla threw her arms around his neck. "Kyla!" her mother scolded.

Kyla put her head down. *It's not the same,* she thought as she fed Chestnut the apple her mom had brought. *Sure wish I could saddle him and ride off where everything would be normal again.*

"Hey, Kyla! You've got company!" Abby called as she ran into the stable.

"Who is it?"

"Megan and Reba."

"Tell them to go away," Kyla said.

"Kyla!" her mother protested.

"I don't want them to see me this way!"

"They won't care," Abby promised.

"But I do." Kyla stomped her foot and lifted her head in frustration. She lowered it before her mother corrected her, but not before she saw Megan and Reba stop abruptly and stare at her.

"We just wanted to see how you were doing," Megan said uneasily.

"Well, get a good look because I'm not going anywhere until this stupid eye heals and I can stand up again," Kyla said. "I feel like an old woman."

"Old women don't have carrot tops," Reba said, trying to lighten the situation.

"Funny. Very funny." Kyla's voice was flat.

"Kyla!" her mother said.

Kyla kicked a bale of straw.

Megan sniffed. "We didn't mean to upset you."

Reba cleared her throat and looked at Megan. "Well, okay, then, guess we'd better go."

Kyla took a deep breath, "Look, I'm sorry to be so grouchy. I just want things to be normal again."

"Yeah, so do we." Kyla heard the hurt in Reba's voice.

"I'll walk you to your car. I want to say hello to Reba's mother," Kyla's mother said.

Mom's apologizing for me, Kyla thought bitterly. *Nobody understands how hard this is!*

WHO TAKES CARE OF YOUR EYES?

- Ophthalmologists are medical doctors who devote themselves to studying the anatomy, function, and diseases of the eye in order to be able to diagnose and treat eye disorders with medical, surgical, or other sophisticated treatments. Some ophthalmologists devote themselves to learning everything they can about certain parts of the eye. They become known as specialists in those areas.
- Retinal specialists are ophthalmologists who have chosen to specialize in becoming experts on diseases of the retina.
- Optometrists are doctors of optometry who examine, diagnose, treat, and manage diseases and disorders of the eye. They check for glaucoma, cataracts, retinal disorders, and test for nearsightedness, farsightedness, astigmatism, and presbyopia. In addition, they prescribe eyeglasses and contact lenses, low-vision aids, vision therapy, and medicines to treat eye diseases.
- Opticians make and sell glasses as prescribed by ophthalmologists or optometrists.

IF I HAVE A VISION PROBLEM, WHAT SHOULD I ASK MY EYE DOCTOR?

- What's my eye condition called?
- What's my central vision?
- What's my side vision?
- Am I likely to lose more vision?
- Are there other tests I should have?
- Are there any surgical options?
- Are there any optical or nonoptical aids that can help me use my remaining vision better?

- Should I have a low-vision evaluation?
- Are there any mobility aids to help me move around more safely?

   (Adapted from www.blindness.org, the Web page of The Foundation Fighting Blindness)

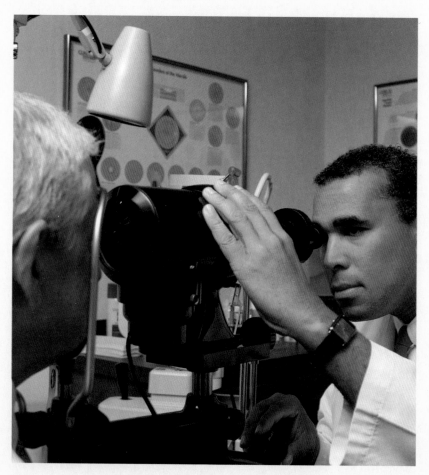

An eye doctor examines a patient's eyes.

Young people with visual impairments ride bicycles with the help of staff members at Camp Abilities.

WORLD-CLASS BLIND TRACK STAR

Blind from the age of ten, Tim Willis won the gold medal in 10,000 meters at the 1998 World Championships held in Berlin, Germany. In 1996, Tim set the world record in the same event in the Colonial Relays at William and Mary College in Virginia. His record for blind runners stood for six years.

This world-class track star started losing his sight when he was in second grade. Three years later, retinal hemorrhages caused by **Coates Disease** left him totally blind. Tim reflects on that time by saying, "I think it's easier to adapt when you're young. Just being normal is the key."

Tim adjusted by learning **Braille**. "That was like learning to read again because you have to learn a whole new set of letters. I'm a strong believer in Braille and use it on a regular basis. For those who are blind, the pathway of learning goes from the ears or the hands to the brain."

Tim also mastered the art of using a white cane so he could get around on his own. He attended Lions Club camps for the blind and participated in Boy Scouts, achieving the rank of Eagle Scout when a sophomore.

In eighth grade, Tim began wrestling. The next year, he started running to train for wrestling. "I wasn't a natural runner," Tim said. "In the beginning, I was the slowest runner on the team. I wanted to improve, so I decided to run every day. To do that, I had to find a guide runner to run with me. We were connected by a shoestring tied around our fingers. His job was to tell me where the turns and competitors were in the race. In high school, my teammates and coaches ran with me. Our high school cross-country team finished fourth in the state."

In college, Tim gave up wrestling but continued to run track and cross-country. He placed fourth in the 1,500 meter and fifth in the 5,000 meter at the 1992 Paralympics (an Olympic-level competition for physically disabled athletes) in Barcelona. In 1996, he won a silver medal in the 10,000 meter and three bronze medals in shorter events.

Two years later, he graduated from college and traveled to Berlin to compete in the World Championships. Tim remembers that as "such a big race for me. It was over 100 degrees that day. Since I had been training in Georgia where it's very hot and humid, the heat worked great for me and I won the gold medal."

Tim continued to compete while at law school. He won a bronze medal in the 10,000 meter and came in fourth in the 5,000 meter at the 2000 Paralympics in Sydney, Australia. He also placed 73rd out of 55,000 in the Peachtree Road Race, the biggest 10K in the world.

Today he practices law in Atlanta, Georgia, fulfilling a boyhood dream. "My grandmother said I wanted to be a lawyer because I liked to argue," Tim said.

Young people who are blind enjoy bowling at Camp Abilities in Brockport, New York.

When asked where he gets his inner strength, Tim said, "My family expected a lot from me. In high school, I was surrounded by high quality teammates who were successful because they worked hard. I had tremendous coaches who believed that if you put forth maximum effort, you might not always win but you would excel. I was always given the opportunity to put forth my best efforts. That had a huge impact on me."

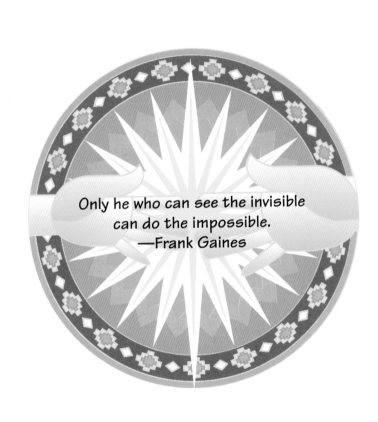

Only he who can see the invisible
can do the impossible.
—Frank Gaines

4

A Jigsaw Puzzle with Some Pieces Missing

On Monday, Kyla's dad got up early to check the maple sap lines before leaving for work. Ryan and Abby boarded the bus for school. Kyla listened as her mother called the office where she worked to request time off to stay home with Kyla.

"I can stay home alone!" Kyla said when her mother hung up the phone. "I'm not sick, and I'm old enough to take care of myself."

Kyla's mom didn't even answer. Instead, she called the school to set up special tutoring for Kyla. Kyla grabbed her jacket and stormed out of the house.

"Kyla!" her mom yelled, running after her. "You can't just go off on your own!"

"Watch me!" Kyla shouted. *Not easy to run with your head down,* she thought as she caught a glimpse of Midnight sprinting toward her. The next second, she slipped on a patch of ice. In a flash, the dog jumped in front of her, breaking her fall. She caught hold of a small tree by the path and managed to right herself. "Thank you, Midnight!" Kyla held onto the tree with one hand while hugging her dog with the other.

"Kyla Elizabeth O'Neill! What were you thinking? You could have ruined everything!" her mom shouted as she ran toward Kyla.

"*Could* have?" Kyla asked. "What are *you* thinking? Everything's already ruined. I can't stand up. I can't see. I can't go to school. I can't even go to the barn alone. My life's one big jigsaw puzzle with half the pieces missing."

"Kyla, honey . . ."

"Don't 'honey' me!"

Kyla's mother backed away. "I'm sorry. I just don't want you to get hurt."

"I don't want to get hurt either! But I'm *not* a baby. I'm almost fourteen! I want to do things myself, not lie around all day." Kyla brushed away her angry tears.

"Fine. But you nearly fell." Kyla's mother reached out to take Kyla's arm. "Let's go call the doctor."

Kyla jerked her arm away. "I didn't get hurt so you don't need to call the doctor! And I'm not coming in!"

"Kyla . . ." Her mother sounded weary, but she didn't argue.

Kyla stomped off to the barn where she threw her arms around her horse. "Oh, Chestnut, what did I do to deserve stupid Humpty-Dumpty eyes that fall apart just playing basketball?" The quarter-horse snorted and nuzzled Kyla. Kyla held him tight, then collapsed on a pile of straw and sobbed.

Two hours later, she woke up feeling something warm and heavy on top of her. "A blanket!" Kyla said as she fingered the texture.

Her mother sat near her, stroking her hair. "Kyla, we're out of milk and bread and—"

"I'm not going to the store," Kyla said.

Her mother stood up. "Well, you're not staying here alone either." Her mother's voice was firm. "I'll drop you off at the library and you can pick out some videos and books on tape."

Kyla fumed as she struggled up the steps to the old stone library. *Sure hope there's nobody here I know!* She tried to find the section with tapes and videos, but it was hard to see with her head down.

Dark green slacks came into view and a voice above them said, "Hi, I'm Francine, the librarian. Could I help you find something?"

"I'm looking for something to listen to while my eye heals."

"Great idea!" Francine pulled several tapes from the shelf and told Kyla about them. Kyla chose a story about a horse and a mystery Francine said was funny.

Preschoolers started coming in for story hour while Kyla sorted through the videos. "What's wrong with her?" a little boy asked.

A little girl pulled on her mother's pants and pointed to Kyla. "Why is she stooped over?"

Kyla clenched her teeth and moved behind bookshelves where the children couldn't see her.

That afternoon Kyla listened to the mystery tape. The day still dragged. When Abby came home, Kyla asked, "Hey, Abby, you want to play Monopoly?"

"Can't," Abby replied. "I'm going to Brandy's to work on a project."

Kyla sighed. *Never thought I'd see the day when I want to play Monopoly and Abby doesn't! It's a funny, upside-down, jigsaw-puzzle world with lots of pieces missing!*

Kyla's dad got home a few minutes later and gave Kyla a peck on the cheek. "Ryan!" he called, "we've got to get the sap boiling."

Kyla sighed. She loved to help make maple syrup. "*Please* let me help."

"Your mother said you fell this morning," her father said.

"I didn't get hurt. And it wouldn't have happened if she hadn't been treating me like a baby."

"She doesn't want you to get hurt," her father said.

"I can't stand that!"

"It's only for three weeks."

"Easy for you to say!"

Her dad cleared his throat.

"So can I come along? I can stoop over in the sap shack just as well as here."

"Okay, Lightning Bug, you win."

"Yes!" Kyla said, jumping up.

"Careful!" her father said.

"Oh, yeah," Kyla said, lowering her head.

Kyla drank in the fresh air as she talked with her dad and Ryan about what a good season it had been for maple syrup. She listened to a woodpecker drill a nearby tree and fed the fire to keep the sap boiling so it would turn into syrup.

"Forty gallons of sap to make one gallon of syrup." Kyla was proud she'd remembered the ratio from previous years.

Ryan went to get more wood, and Kyla told her dad about the kids at the library. "They're young," he said. "They didn't mean any harm."

"I know, but that's what everybody thinks, too. Kids just say what everyone else is thinking."

"There's no such thing as 'what everybody thinks' because different people see things differently. Besides, you'll drive yourself crazy if you live worrying about what other people think," her father said. "You just have to be the best you can be with what life gives you."

"Yeah, well I don't like what life's giving me! It's not fair! What did I ever do to deserve bad eyes?"

"You didn't do anything, Kyla."

"Then why do I have them? Why would God do this to me?"

"Kyla," her dad said, stroking her hair. "I wish I knew."

Kyla's tutor, Mrs. Bartelle, arrived on Tuesday armed with textbooks and assignment sheets. She went over the vocabulary words Kyla's class was studying in English, discussed a social studies assignment, showed Kyla how to do her math problems, and helped her with a science experiment.

When Mrs. Bartelle left, Kyla worked on her math for an hour. Kyla wrote sentences for her vocabulary words and then tried to read her social studies. *The print is really small,* Kyla thought as she nodded off.

The next day, Mrs. Bartelle checked Kyla's homework. When Kyla repeatedly said, "Oh, I thought that was a three," or "Oh, that's a seven?" Mrs. Bartelle offered to enlarge her assignments. She also suggested that they tape Kyla's classes so she could keep up without too much reading.

The next two and a half weeks became a jigsaw puzzle where Kyla pieced the frame together with the routines of homework, meals, tapes, and videos. She filled in the middle with special activities like making maple syrup, building a hump-backed snowman with Abby, listening for the honking of the Canadian geese as they returned north, finding yellow crocuses and daffodils on her way to visit Chestnut, and playing the piano.

Kyla worried about how she'd treated her friends and whether she'd be able to see when her eye healed. Her worries left dark circles under her eyes . . . and she felt like her fears were driving holes in her heart. She called Megan, but their conversation was filled with long, awkward pauses.

Kyla's return visit to Dr. Goodwin didn't go much better.

"Your eye is healing well," he told her after many tests, "but you've lost most of your central vision."

"So, I'm blind," Kyla said.

"Your right eye's about 20/70 with your contacts in, but the vision in your left eye is only 20/200, meaning you're legally blind in that eye."

"Can't I just get stronger contacts?"

"You remember what I told you about myopia and macular degeneration?"

"Contacts correct myopia, but they don't help with the other problem." Kyla swallowed hard.

"Right."

"So I'm going to have to live with stupid Humpty-Dumpty eyes the rest of my life."

"For right now. There is a lot of research being done and there may be something to help you some day, maybe even soon," Dr. Goodwin said.

Kyla looked at the floor and kicked the leg of her chair.

"It won't be easy, Kyla, but there are things you can do. My staff will give you information about low-vision specialists and organizations to help you." He cleared his throat and took Kyla's hand. "You, Miss O'Neill, are a beautiful, brilliant young lady with a marvelous sense of humor. With determination, you can do almost anything you want to do. Your visual impairment is only one small part of who you are. Never let it limit your potential or define who you are."

Kyla nodded, forced a little smile, took her father's arm, and stumbled out of the doctor's office. *Easy for you to say!* she thought.

WHAT DO THE TERMS MEAN?

Visual impairment refers to the loss of vision rather than to the actual disorder that causes it. The degree of impairment is often given in numbers based on the Snellen eye chart. If you can see what most people see when twenty feet from the chart, you have 20/20 vision. If you can read at twenty feet what most people can read at one hundred feet, you have 20/100 vision.

According to the National Information Center for Children and Youth with Disabilities, 12.2 out of every 1,000 young people under the age of 18 have visual impairments.

The following terms are sometimes used to describe the degree of impairment:

- Partially sighted means there is a visual problem for which some adaptations or special education may be needed.
- Low vision suggests there is a severe visual impairment with distance or close vision even when glasses or contact lenses are worn. Special lighting, large print materials, and books on tape may be required. Computers with enlarged letters and low-vision optical and video aids may also be needed. Learning to use the other senses and residual vision efficiently is important. Braille may occasionally be suggested.
- Legally blind refers to vision that is less than 20/200 in the better eye when corrected. It is also used when the field of vision is limited to less than twenty degrees at its widest point. Adaptations as above will be required. It is also important to develop the skills needed to get around safely, perform the activities of

daily living, and prepare for a vocation. Braille may be useful.

- Totally blind indicates that there is no usable vision. Braille or other nonvisual media, mobility skills with a cane or guide dog, and adapted living skills are essential.

(Adapted from material from the National Information Center for Children and Youth with Disabilities, www.nichcy.org)

A student at Batavia School for the Blind reads his schoolwork with his fingers.

BRAILLE: BAFFLING OR BENEFICIAL?

Does Braille baffle you?

You're not alone. For those who don't understand it, Braille looks and feels like a mysterious secret code of bumps that make no sense. Yet many people have mastered Braille and read two hundred to four hundred words a minute, a rate print readers would be proud to do.

For those with severe visual loss, Braille opens up the worlds of literature, philosophy, history, and religion and becomes a tool for studying math, science, spelling, foreign languages, law, music, and many other disciplines. Braille readers say the only problem with Braille is that there isn't enough material available.

How does it work?

- A Braille cell consists of six raised dots arranged in two parallel rows of three dots each.
- Letters, numbers, punctuation marks, and words are created by specific combinations of raised dots within a Braille cell.
- Dot positions are identified by numbers from one to six.
- Sixty-four different configurations can be made by using one or more of the dots.

Two different forms of Braille are used:

- Grade 1 or uncontracted Braille means that every letter of every word is spelled in Braille.
- Grade 2 refers to contracted Braille, a system of shortcuts whereby cells are used individually or in combination with others to form a variety of contractions or whole words. This saves paper and speeds up the reading process. One hundred eighty-

nine different letter contractions and seventy-six short-form words are used. Most written material uses Grade 2 Braille.

Braille can be written with

- a *stylus* and slate
- a *Braillewriter*
- an electronic Braille note taker. Electronic devices allow material to be saved and edited, displayed verbally or *tactually*, and produced in hard copy using a desktop computer-driven Braille *embosser*.

HOW WAS BRAILLE INVENTED?

Louis Braille was a teenager when he and some of his friends at the National Institute for Blind Youth in Paris discovered they could read and write with raised dots quicker than with raised print letters. Braille worked on modifying a code used for sending military messages at night to create a cell of six dots from which an alphabet and number system could be created.

In 1820, when only eighteen, Braille finished developing the system that bears his name. It took more than a century for people to accept Braille as an important way to communicate. Those who use it are grateful for the countless hours of enjoyment and intellectual stimulation the system gives them.

The National Federation of the Blind (NFB) believes that instruction in Braille should be available to every child with a severe visual handicap if the parents want it.

The NFB states, "No child is hurt by learning Braille, print, or any other skill. A federal law is often cited as the excuse for not making Braille universally available to the blind, but the law is misquoted. The requirement that each child's individual

a	b	c	d	e	f	g	h	i	j
(1)	(2)	(3)	(4)	(5)	(6)	(7)	(8)	(9)	(0)

k	l	m	n	o	p	q	r	s	t

u	v	w	x	y	z

mother	
much	mch
must	mst
myself	myf

about	ab
above	abv
according	ac
across	acr
after	af
afternoon	afn
afterward	afw
again	ag
against	agst
ally	
almost	alm
already	alr
also	al
although	alth
altogether	alt
always	alw
ance	
and	
ar	
as	
ation	

cc	
ch	
character	
child	
children	chn
com	
con	
conceive	concv
conceiving	concvg
could	cd
day	
dd	
deceive	dcv
deceiving	dcvg
declare	dcl
declaring	dclg
dis	
do	

from	
ful	
gg	
gh	
go	
good	gd
great	grt
had	
have	
here	
herself	herf
him	hm
himself	hmf
his	
immediate	imm
in	
ing	
into	

name	
necessary	nec
neither	nei
ness	
not	
o'clock	o'c
of	
one	
oneself	onef
ong	
ou	
ought	
ound	
ount	
ourselves	ourvs
out	

A Braille chart.

needs be met was never meant as a cop-out for teachers and an excuse for illiteracy. Just as with the sighted, the blind need every skill we can get to compete in today's world. With proper training, we can hold our own with the best."

For them, Braille's benefit far outweighs its bafflement.

HOW WOULD THINGS LOOK IF I HAD AN EYE DISORDER?

- Cataracts cloud the lenses and lead to hazy vision with a lack of visual acuity or sharpness of detail.
- Diabetic retinopathy means that the retina, macula, or vitreous are deteriorating because of changes caused by diabetes. The loss of vision usually develops gradually. Cataracts are also more common with diabetes.
- Glaucoma indicates there is chronic elevated pressure in the eye that may cause a loss of peripheral vision.
- Hemianopia, or vision loss in half of the field of vision, may occur after a stroke, tumor, or trauma.
- Macular degeneration decreases central vision and visual acuity.
- Retinitis pigmentosa involves night blindness and a severe loss of peripheral or side vision due to congenital degeneration of cells in the retina.
  (Information adapted from Lighthouse International.)

GOOD NEWS FOR BLIND MUSICIANS

Braille music provides the information a sighted person gets from a page of print music. This allows a blind musician to work through piano, band, or choral parts; study music theory; take sight-singing classes; and analyze music scores—skills necessary for music majors.

The largest source of Braille music is the music section of the National Library Service, Library of Congress, but other resources are also available.

The National Resource Center for Blind Musicians provides information and referral services to help:

- musicians who are losing their vision find new ways to reach their goals
- teachers assist students who are visually impaired or blind
- find Braille music
- provide training in Braille music and technology in on-site workshops in New York and New England
- students studying music at the college level acquire skills through an intensive residential program known as the Summer Institute for Blind College-bound Musicians
  (Information adapted from the National Resource Center for Blind Musicians.)

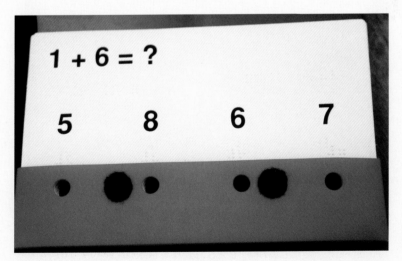

Braille flashcards are used to help young students learn their math facts.

A Braille ruler.

SEEING THE WORLD THROUGH MUSIC

Jermaine Gardner was born with hypertelorism, a rare disease that caused marked facial deformity and blocked the formation of one of his eyes while leaving the other sealed shut.

"When I saw him, I freaked out. I cursed God and wanted to die. I called my mother and screamed, 'I don't want to see him anymore. He's blind and his face is disfigured. You can tell my friends he died,'" his mother, Jacqui, said.

"These are the children we hold dear. We don't give our children away. We bring them home and nurture them," Jacqui's mother replied.

Jacqui says, "Her words were just what I needed to put an end to my pity party."

For the next six months, Jermaine gave evidence of having light perception. Doctors tried three corneal transplants, but Jermaine's body rejected them. In the midst of the problems, Jacqui's sister told her, "God has given you a gift."

"How can you say that? I have this blind kid with this horrible face. People stare at me. I don't know what to do," Jacqui said.

But the next week, when Jermaine's four-year-old brother practiced the piano, Jacqui put Jermaine's fingers on the keys. To her amazement, Jermaine began playing the same song his brother was playing. Jacqui noticed Jermaine also began smiling, something he'd never done before. Then he threw his head back and played with intensity.

Soon Jermaine insisted on playing the piano all the time. "We had to feed him at the piano, change him at the piano, and wait until he fell asleep at the piano to put him to bed. The next morning we'd start all over again," Jacqui recalls. "He was playing Bach and Beethoven by the time he was two."

In 1987, ABC News included Jermaine in a story featuring child geniuses. A team of doctors saw the story and called to say they could repair his facial deformity.

While Jermaine continued to play the piano, he also learned to play many other instruments. Everyone who heard him marveled at his extraordinary gift. Everyone but Jermaine, that is. His comment on coming home from fifth grade one day revealed how surprised he was that other kids weren't just like him: "Hey, Mom, did you know some people don't play the piano?"

To a large degree, that's how Jermaine views his blindness, too. "Sometimes it goes back and forth and can be annoying. But I've never seen. So I just do what I have to do. If I were to see now, I'd probably have to learn to play all over again."

This computer has a Braille keyboard, as well as a Braille monitor display.

A Braillewriter looks a little like a typewriter.

Whether or not that's true, Jermaine's talent continues to amaze others. He has produced two CDs and is now studying at the Oberlin Music Conservatory. Before enrolling at Oberlin, Jermaine attended the National Resource Center for Blind Musicians where he learned to read Braille music.

"It was one of the most important things I ever did," he said. "I learned so much in two weeks. Now I can read music and interpret it myself instead of just learning it by ear."

Poor eyes limit your sight;
poor vision limits your deeds.
—Franklin Field

5

THE SEA MONSTER

Kyla cried all the way home. What good had it done to keep her head down? Memories bounced around inside her head like rubber balls.

What's the matter, Carrot-top? You blind?

What's wrong with her?

The game always ended with, *You're blind, Carrot-top! That's what's wrong.*

Kyla had looked forward to going back to school. Now she dreaded it. How would she get to her classes on time? See the board? Keep up with her assignments? Take gym? Would her teachers get mad at her? Would her friends understand? Or would they just think she was a dork?

When the alarm rang on Monday morning, Kyla struggled to wake up, then staggered to the bathroom, bumping into the door. "Who left the door half open?" she yelled.

After her shower, she rummaged through her closet three times before finding the shirt she wanted. She never found the right color socks.

"You're going to be late!" her mother called.

Kyla grabbed her sneakers and ran downstairs, slipping on the last two steps. She grabbed the banister and muttered, "That's it for dumb things for today. Slow down and watch what you're doing, Kyla O'Neill!"

Her mother handed her an English muffin. "Eat this on the way. I've got your books."

Kyla and her mother stopped at the principal's office to fill out forms related to Kyla's injury. "We'll set up an appointment with the vision support team to see that Kyla gets the special services she needs," Mrs. Royer said.

"Special services?" Kyla asked. "What kind of special services?"

"Things to help you with your vision problem. Our **mobility instructor**, Mrs. Hartman, is here right now to help you find the best way to your classes," Mrs. Royer said.

"I don't need help finding my classes!" Kyla said. "And I don't need special services. I'm not stupid!" Kyla gripped her books and stomped out the door.

"Kyla!" her mother said, ready to rush after her.

"Let's see how she makes out," Mrs. Hartman said.

Kyla hadn't been in the hall fifteen seconds before she wondered if she'd made a mistake. Bodies pushed and shoved, cut in and out in front of her like a writhing sea monster ready to devour its victim—her. Kyla quickly moved to the wall. *At least the wall doesn't move!*

But sometimes wall-hugging groups in front of her didn't move either, and she had to merge back into mid-hall traffic. At times, she heard kids ask each other, "Is that Kyla?" but she couldn't see their faces well enough to know who they were.

Kyla turned left, then right, but she couldn't read room numbers and keep from being run over at the same time.

When the bell rang for classes to begin, Kyla found herself near the library. She leaned against the wall and took a deep breath. *That was awful! But I still don't want everybody watching me be led to classes by a mobility instructor.*

Jeremy Jordan came rushing around a corner. "Well, if it isn't Kyla the Carrot-top come back to school!"

Kyla closed her eyes and sucked in her breath.

"Hey, Basketball Queen, you need some help?" he asked.

"Not from you, Jerko!"

"Just thought you might be going to math class and I could use you as a pass to get in. But, maybe you're in some different class—some higher class—some *special* class now."

Kyla bristled. "No special classes!" she said and followed Jeremy to class.

Mr. Ferdinand was already explaining an equation he'd put on the board when Kyla and Jeremy entered. "Mr. Jordan, you're late. Again. Do you have a pass?"

"Better than that, Mr. Ferdinand. I rescued Kyla. Surely that should count for more than some little slip of paper."

"I believe she is also late," Mr. Ferdinand said.

Kyla stared at the floor. *So much for not attracting attention.*

"Miss O'Neill, since this is your first day back, I'll overlook your tardiness today. Now please be seated."

The only empty seat Kyla could find was near the back in the row by the windows. She tripped over a backpack trying to get there. The class snickered. Mr. Ferdinand cleared his throat. Kyla sank into the seat and strained to see what Mr. Ferdinand was writing on the board. Was he using invisible chalk?

When the buzzer between classes sounded, Kyla didn't know whether to laugh or cry. Surely English class would go better . . . but she'd have to fight her way through the hall to get there. Kyla realized she didn't remember the room number, even though she *knew* where her English class should be; she just didn't know how to get there anymore. She held her schedule close to her eyes to check the room number. Room 116. That shouldn't be too bad.

Mrs. Avalon welcomed Kyla and told everyone how well she'd kept up with her homework while recovering at home after surgery. Kyla appreciated the praise but sensed an odd silence in the class. *Was it sympathy? Jealousy? Or something worse?* Kyla tried to shrug it off and concentrate on the vocabulary drills.

History class was only four doors away. Mr. Wiley lectured at his usual machine-gun pace, and Kyla struggled to take notes. She couldn't see what she was writing, though. How would she ever be able to read these later? Or the chapter he'd assigned for homework?

When the class finished, Kyla waited until Megan came by. "Hey, Megan, can I walk to gym class with you?"

"We'll have to hurry," Megan said. "Ms. Nellerino's not big on people being late."

Not as friendly as I'd hoped, Kyla thought. She struggled to keep up with Megan as she snaked her way through the hall. *Better than being alone, though.*

One foot inside the locker room, Kyla realized she'd forgotten her gym clothes. "You can keep score," Ms. Nellerino told her.

Kyla loved volleyball. But she didn't like keeping score—especially when she couldn't always see the ball or the boundary lines. She had to watch how the teams reacted to decide who got the point. That worked for a while, but then Reba insisted the ball had gone out of bounds when Kyla had given the other team a point. "You blind or what?" Reba called.

Kyla took a deep breath and ducked her head. Ms. Nellerino stopped the game and lectured Reba—and everyone else—on sportsmanship.

Kyla swallowed hard, feeling she'd gotten everyone in trouble.

Megan confirmed her suspicions as Kyla walked to the locker room with her. "That was a bad call, Kyla."

"Sorry. I did the best I could."

"Well, it's not fair for all of us to get yelled at because you can't see straight."

Stunned, Kyla leaned against a locker and bit her bottom lip to hold back tears.

Someone she'd never met stuck out her hand. "Hi, I'm Emily. I'm new here. Just need to get my stuff out of that locker."

"Sorry," Kyla said.

"You new, too?"

"No. I had eye surgery. My name's Kyla."

"Where you headed?"

"Lunch, I think. What about you?"

"Same." Emily paused. "My gram's blind."

"I'm sorry."

"Don't be too sorry. Gram wouldn't like it. She lives with us now. But she still cooks and bakes and knits and crochets. And tells stories." Emily shifted her books. "I love her stories."

"My left eye's legally blind, but I still have some side vision. And I can see with my right eye, except things are blurry in the middle."

"I'll bet getting around this place is a nightmare."

"You better believe it!" Kyla smiled for the first time all day.

Emily was easy to follow. She steered Kyla through the hazards of hall traffic with funny comments, then helped find a shelf to stash Kyla's books so they could navigate the lunch line. "Macaroni and cheese—pretty good. Steak sandwiches—like shoe leather. Carrot sticks, celery with peanut butter, applesauce—always safe. Red Jell-O—eat at your own risk."

Kyla laughed at her new friend's quiet commentary and let her lead the way to an open table. She discovered Emily had moved to Maple Grove from New Jersey, that she had an older brother named Carter, liked to swim, and loved to act.

On Emily's way to history class, she walked Kyla to science class and promised to meet Kyla again in chorus.

Miss Clark handed out outlines on the ozone layer. She spoke softly as she drew diagrams on the board. Kyla tried desperately to see and take notes, but eventually she fell asleep from the effort. When she woke up, she scanned the class to see if there was anyone who could help her . . . with science or with getting to her next class. Things looked hopeless on both scores.

When the buzzer sounded, Kyla took a deep breath and exited with the class. In seconds, she felt swallowed by the seething student sea monster slithering through the hall. Two boys stopped abruptly right in front of her. She crashed into them. "Sorry!" she said.

"Just wanted to see if the Carrot-top was still blind." They laughed.

She had just rounded a corner when a tall, skinny kid cut in front of her and opened his locker door. Kyla swerved to the left, bumping into some girls who shouted, "Hey, watch it!"

Kyla murmured, "Sorry!" again and looked up to see where she was. The sign said "Health Office." She ducked inside.

"Feeling sick?" The nurse handed her a clipboard so she could sign in.

"I've gotten smashed twice in the last thirty seconds and must have taken a wrong turn," Kyla replied. "But other than that . . ."

The nurse looked up. "Oh, Kyla! You had eye surgery, right?"

"Yes," Kyla said.

"Having trouble seeing?"

"Some."

"I'll call special services," the nurse said.

"No!" Kyla stormed back into the hall, determined to find the chorus room herself. She paused, trying to remember which way to go.

"Over here, Kyla!" a friendly voice to her left called.

Emily led her into the chorus room. "Saved you a seat right by me. Hope you're an alto."

Kyla let out a deep breath. "I will be today—as long as you help me find the notes!"

IS THERE ANYTHING YOU CAN DO TO HELP PREVENT VISION LOSS?

How you eat and what you do when you're young may affect how you see when you're older!

No one wants to lose his or her sight. Researchers constantly do studies to determine what role nutrition and environmental factors play in the development of age-related macular degeneration (AMD), currently the leading cause of blindness for those over 55. Here are some tips for decreasing your risk of AMD:

- Eat lots of fresh fruits and vegetables, especially the green, leafy ones like spinach, kale, and collard greens.
- Eat at least two servings of fish per week.
- Avoid fats found in snack foods like potato chips, French fries, cakes, and commercially prepared pies.
- Don't smoke! Two separate studies found that smokers were twice as likely to develop AMD.
- Wear UV absorbing lenses and a hat that shades the eyes when in the sun as prolonged exposure to the sun may damage the macula.

    (Adapted from information from the Age-Related Eye Disease study (AREDS) and the Foundation Fighting Blindness, www.blindness.org)

A BLIND JOKE A DAY

Most people find it challenging to cope with one visual problem. Doug Webber lives with four!

Doug experienced a detached retina when he was six, followed by cataracts, glaucoma, and macular degeneration. To adapt in school, Doug began using the Jordy system. He explains it this way: "I wear a head mounted device with a camera on it. Two screens right in front of my eyes display what the camera sees. That allows me to zoom in on the blackboard or a textbook and complete my assignments."

Knowing how precarious his sight is, Doug also became proficient in Braille. He was a National Merit Scholar, an all-conference swimmer, and was the captain of his swim team for three years. Doug is currently pursuing a double major in economics and political science at the University of Florida. His ultimate goal? "To earn my PhD and teach at a university."

Doug faces his visual impairment head on. "One thing I try to do every day is make fun of my vision. I will make a blind joke any chance I get. This lets people know that I am not uptight about my vision and that if they have any questions, I am willing to answer them."

When asked where he gets his inner strength, Doug says, "I've always tried to be the best I can be and never used my vision as a crutch to lean on."

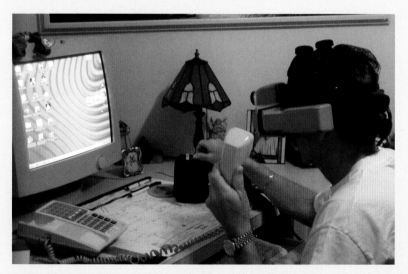

This man is using the Jordy system to read the computer monitor.

Young people who are blind or visually impaired can still enjoy sports.

LET THE GOLD RUB OFF!

When she was a child, Beth Scott met an Olympic gold medallist who didn't want anyone to touch her medal because it might get tarnished. Beth decided she would never be that way if she became a champion athlete. "I want the gold to rub off, to inspire dreams in young people," she says.

Born with two rare genetic eye disorders that normally affect only boys, Beth faced a dark future. Ocular albinism stripped her retina of its normal pigment, leaving her legally blind. Nystagmus affected the nerves and muscles behind her eyes, resulting in irregular, rapid eye movements.

Beth faced many surgeries as a child and found school difficult. She started swimming at age five. When she was eight, she learned the butterfly stroke and began winning competitions. "I didn't have to read anything but the time

Like many young people, this student at the Batavia School for the Blind enjoys using the computer to learn. He bends close to see the large symbols on the special keypad.

clock and I felt equal to everyone else in the water. When I wore goggles, no one saw my nystagmus."

By 1992, Beth was ranked sixth in the nation in the 200-meter butterfly. She missed making the Olympic team by just half a second. By accident, she discovered she could compete in the Paralympics. "I thought this was just something for poor, disabled folks and had never thought of myself as disabled. But it was a chance to swim, so I agreed to compete and convinced officials to let me train with the Olympic swimmers in Colorado Springs since I would be representing the United States.

"It was an eye-opening experience that changed my life. I'd never been around people who were visually impaired. People were so welcoming and helpful. I roomed with Marla Runyan, an outstanding runner, and made friends with great people from around the world."

Kids with visual impairments and blindness learn to swim at Camp Abilities.

Staff members at Camp Abilities help a camper learn to bowl.

Beth swam very well, winning seven gold medals and setting seven world records. As she flew home, she looked at the sunset and said, "This was a really cool three weeks." Then she looked at her medals and said, "God, for years I prayed my problem would go away. Now I realize that my disability's not a curse but a blessing. I really am an athlete and I've had a chance to meet many people with similar problems."

Beth looks on that time as her "awakening at age 17." She changed her major from interior design to adapted physical education so she could help others with similar problems.

Beth has won many other medals and awards, including being chosen by the United States Olympic Committee as the Blind Athlete of the Year in 1993 and 1996. She retired from competitive swimming after the Sydney games in 2000 because she found she had thyroid cancer. She moved to the Washington-Baltimore area to work at the National Institutes of Health in child health and development while she wages a battle against cancer. "Things sometimes take a long time to work out and don't always work out as you think," Beth says.

Despite the setback, Beth continues to tackle new challenges with an optimistic attitude and works to inspire young people. Beth's never forgotten her promise. So, if you meet her, ask to see her medals. If she has them with her, she'll be happy to let you finger them so the gold can rub off!

Of course, she may expect you to share the gold in your life, too!

Young people who are visually impaired enjoy a modified version of softball.

Vision does not come by inspiration.
It comes from knowledge. . . .
—Robert A. Weaver

6

You're Gonna Make It, Lightning Bug!

When she got home from school on Friday afternoon, Kyla threw her books on the floor and collapsed on the family-room sofa. *Why did I ever think that going back to school would make life normal again?* Except for Emily, the week had been wretched.

Her mom had returned to work on Tuesday, forcing Kyla to take the bus, a torture chamber of harassment all its own. She'd failed tests in math, history, and science but continued to be Mrs. Avalon's pet, much to everyone's annoyance. Megan and her friends avoided her. *I can't go on like this!* Kyla thought as a torrent of tears dissolved the brittle shell she'd built around herself.

Outside she heard Ryan and his buddies roar into the driveway in Matt's stripped-down jalopy. "Look at those wheels, man!" "Hey, listen to that motor rev!" "I hear you're gonna paint it purple!" she heard as they inspected the old pickup Ryan had bought with his birthday money.

Only two more years until I can get my license too— Kyla stopped mid-thought. *What if I'm never able to drive?* She closed her eyes and punched the sofa.

Kyla stayed in bed until ten the next morning, then pulled on a sweatshirt and jeans, ate a handful of cereal, grabbed her jacket, and headed out. The sunshine's glare on the snow hurt her eyes. Reluctantly, she went back inside and got sunglasses, then followed the smell of the wood fire to the maple-syrup shed.

"Good afternoon!" her dad called.

"Very funny!" Kyla inhaled the aroma of the sap turning to syrup.

"How was your week, Lightning Bug?"

Kyla sighed. "If you knew, you wouldn't ask."

"That bad?"

"Worse." Kyla blinked away a tear.

That afternoon, Kyla struggled to read her history assignment and worked on math. It was all she could do to make out the words and numbers even with her nose nearly touching the pages. Eventually, she dozed off on top of her books.

She jumped when the phone rang. "Hi, this is Emily," the voice in her ear said when she picked up the phone.

"Emily?" Kyla was still too sleepy to make sense out of what was happening.

"The Emily you've been eating lunch with all week. Remember me?"

"Oh yeah. Of course I do! Look, I'm really sorry. Really, really sorry. Guess I fell asleep doing homework, and I answered the phone before my brain woke up!"

"It's okay," Emily said. "Been there; done that myself. I was just wondering if you'd like to come over tomorrow?"

"Love to!" Kyla was excited about something for the first time since she'd been injured.

Emily's brother Carter picked up Kyla the next morning. He helped Kyla in the car, then turned it around in their driveway. *Even I can see he's tall, dark, and handsome,* Kyla thought.

At dinner, Emily told Gram: "Your meat loaf is at twelve

o'clock, your mashed potatoes are at three o'clock, your green beans are at six o'clock, and your coleslaw is at nine o'clock. I've buttered your roll and put it on a little plate above your knife."

Dinner conversation covered everything from Gram's incredible cinnamon buns to Carter's skydiving. Gram told stories from her childhood that made everyone laugh.

After dessert, Kyla closed her eyes while Emily handed her some coins. Kyla identified the quarters easily but had trouble knowing whether the rest were pennies, nickels, or dimes. When Emily handed her some paper money, Kyla thought she was kidding when she asked her if the bills were ones, fives, tens, or twenties. "Now ask Gram," Emily told Kyla.

Gram aced the test.

"How'd she do that?" Kyla asked.

"Ask her," Emily said.

Kyla blushed. "I'm sorry, Mrs. Norris. I just treated you the same way kids treat me at school. I hate it when they talk about me as if I'm not there."

Gram smiled. "Have they started raising their voices or talking real slow to you yet?"

Kyla shook her head. "Don't tell me I have that to look forward to."

Gram smiled. "Maybe you'll be lucky."

"So how do you know what money's what?"

"Dimes are the smallest and have ridged edges. Nickels are bigger and thicker. Pennies are in between and have smooth edges. I keep my ones flat, my fives folded in half, my tens folded in quarters, and my twenties folded in triangles."

"Cool!"

Carter cleared the table so Emily could show Kyla around the house. "Gram's room's the neatest," Emily said. "She has things labeled with Braille dots so she knows what's what and she color codes her clothes."

"Hurry up! We're ready to play Scrabble," Gram called.

Kyla shook her head. "No way!"

Emily smiled. "Gram has a special board with Braille letters in the corners of the tiles. See if you can beat her."

No one did. Not even Carter.

On Monday, Kyla started the school routine again. That afternoon, she was called to the office. Her heart skipped a beat when she saw her parents and several other adults seated around a table. Her father held out a chair for her and said, "Kyla, this is part of the vision support team."

Kyla felt betrayed.

The team explained that they wanted to help her stay in her regular classes and live as normally as possible. She would be seated where she could best see the board and be given copies of what was on the board or allowed to copy another student's notes. She could have extra time to take tests. If she needed them, she could have large-print books, tests, worksheets, and notes; bold-lined paper; black pens, pencils, and markers. She could also request raised maps, a four-track tape recorder, a *closed-circuit TV* with a reading stand, and other *optical aids*.

Mrs. Hartman would show Kyla techniques to protect herself in the halls and special ways to get around. Kyla would be allowed to leave classes five minutes early so she wouldn't have to fight hall traffic. She would be able to have alternative activities in gym or take *adaptive physical education classes* where she could participate in activities such as swimming and track. She could also play basketball, soccer, kick ball, volleyball, and baseball with balls equipped with beepers or bells. She could learn Braille and have a Braillewriter and Braille books if she needed them.

Most importantly, she would be taught to use her *residual vision* wisely and would be involved in deciding what she needed.

"What do you think, Kyla?" her father asked.

Kyla bit her bottom lip. "I didn't want to look stupid by having special services, but now I see I'd be stupid not to try them."

Her dad put his arm around her and wiped tears from both their eyes as he said, "You're gonna make it, Lightning Bug."

LOW-VISION RESOURCES

Eyeglasses, medicine, and surgery correct most visual problems. However, people who still have trouble reading, recognizing others, or seeing objects and potential obstacles such as steps, curbs, walls, and furniture—even after seeking correction—are experiencing problems with low vision.

Low vision is sometimes called usable vision. Ophthalmologists and optometrists who specialize in low-vision care perform extensive tests to determine visual function so they can recommend low-vision devices that would be the most useful in individual cases.

Many low-vision devices are available. Here are a few of them:

- half glasses with reading prisms
- microscopes
- reading telescopes
- handheld monocle and/or binoculars
- absorptive lenses
- stand magnifiers
- hand magnifiers

Other adaptive devices include

- large-print clocks, timers, calculators, remote controls, watches, books
- large-print crossword puzzles, dominoes, playing cards
- computer or television screen magnifiers
- bold felt-tipped pens
- signature and writing guides
- talking watches, clocks, calculators, daily organizers, tape measures
- talking scales, heart rate monitors, thermometers
- talking pedometers, message recorders, VCR players

- beep balls such as footballs, soccer balls, and softballs
- computer games
- magnified mirrors
- sewing aids
- Braille watches, books, music, translation software
- Braille board games such as Scrabble, Monopoly, and bingo

A young blind student learns about the parts of a bean seed using special teaching materials that allow him to look with his fingers.

These teaching materials are designed especially for students who are visually impaired.

IS THERE HOPE FOR THE FUTURE?

Researchers are working hard to find ways to cure the diseases that destroy sight and to restore vision through surgery or new treatments. Some exciting possibilities include:

- retinal cell transplants
- pharmaceutical therapy
- nutritional therapy
- gene therapy
- high-tech auto-focus glasses
- retinal microchips to create a "bionic eye"

SPACE ENGINEER WITH STARGARDT'S

NASA engineer Paul Mogan began bumping into things when he was three. His diagnosis? Stargardt's, a syndrome not usually seen until the early teens.

In school, Paul struggled to see the chalkboard and used bifocal and other magnifiers to read. He felt clumsy when attempting to play baseball or other sports and found it hard to fit in. Classified as legally blind while in high school, Paul was not allowed to drive. Although very disappointed, Paul says, "I had to come to terms with it and realize that I am not defined by my circumstances; I am defined by who I choose to be."

As he reflects on his high school days, he says, "I didn't have many friends because I was unhappy with who I was, but I never really understood that until later. It's important to show people you're just a regular person who has to do things a little differently. Give people time to get used to the differences and be willing to talk with them about your eye problems.

"Self doubt is the greatest enemy we have. Believing there's a way to overcome challenges and do well is about 90 percent of the battle. The rest is mostly a matter of working smart, finding the right tools (visual aids, software, etc.) and working hard."

In 1999, he began using a vision-enhancing system based on NASA technology. Dubbed "Jordy" after a blind Star Trek Next Generation character who uses a special visor to help him see, the system allowed Paul to increase his vision level from five percent of what an average person sees to 20/20. Because it was bulky, however, it caused considerable neck strain when worn for extended periods.

Dr. Scott Hearing, one of the developers of the Jordy system, invited Paul to put his engineering background and long-standing experience with poor vision to work in

This machine magnifies the words on the page and displays them on a monitor, enabling a visually impaired person to read.

helping to evaluate and improve the system. His input helped launch a streamlined version known as Jordy 2, which weighs less and focuses better. Because of the progress made in the last five years, Dr. Hearing predicts that Jordy 2-type technology may soon be developed to look like ordinary glasses.

Thanks to the Jordy system, Paul has enjoyed a successful career with NASA for sixteen years.

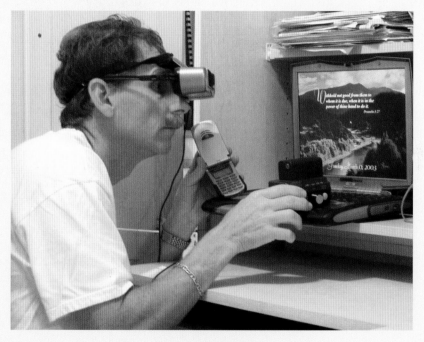

The Jordy system.

The best and most beautiful things in the world
cannot be seen . . . but are felt in the heart.
—Helen Keller

7

New Horizons Camp

Accepting the recommendations of the vision teachers helped Kyla finish the year with reasonably good grades. She still struggled with many activities and felt left out at times because she was different. Even so, she was shocked when her parents signed her up for New Horizons Camp for the Blind that summer. "I'm not blind!" she told them.

"You've been given a scholarship, and we want you to try it," they told her.

They dropped her off at camp late in June. Thunderclouds darkened the sky, matching her attitude. She dragged her duffle bag into Cabin #3 and sank down on the bunk.

"Hey! You sat on me!" a voice shouted. Kyla jumped.

"Sorry! I didn't know anybody was here." Kyla looked around the cabin. "There aren't any lights on."

"Don't need lights when you're blind."

"Never thought of that," Kyla said. *I can see this will be a fun week!* "I'm Kyla," she said, sticking out her hand.

"Shandra," the dark person on the bunk said, not responding to Kyla's outstretched hand. *Oh, yeah, she can't see my hand!* Kyla withdrew her hand, feeling foolish.

"Mind if I turn on the lights so I can put away my stuff?" Kyla asked.

"Light . . . dark . . . all the same to me," Shandra said. "Guess you can still see."

"Some. You been blind long?"

"Born that way," Shandra said.

"Sorry."

"Yeah. Not fun."

"How do you get around?" Kyla asked.

"Cane."

"Do you have any idea what you look like?"

"Black hair, black eyes, black skin, red lips, white teeth."

With her side vision, Kyla looked at Shandra. "How do you know that?"

"I've got sources."

"How do you fix your hair?"

"Hands." Shandra cleared her throat. "Now, Miss Question Box, let's hear about you."

"Sorry," Kyla said. "I didn't mean to pry."

"No problem. Around here, we all share our stories."

Kyla had just started telling Shandra about her accident when a voice said, "Hi, I'm Carmina, your cabin counselor. I'm glad you're all here." Carmina added, "This is my **_guide dog_**, Scout. When he has his harness on, he knows he's on the job working as my eyes. Please don't talk to him or play with him then. When I take off his harness at night, he's off duty. He'd love to have you play with him then."

Carmina turned to the girls who were with her. "This is Lauren and Nadia. Lauren's thirteen and has Stargardt's, an inherited form of juvenile macular degeneration. She's a great runner. Nadia's fifteen. She lost her eyesight to cancer when she was six. You'll hear her using her Braillewriter to journal everything we do at camp because she loves to write."

Carmina paused. "Okay, I'm not sure where you are, Shandra the shark swimmer, but I know you're here someplace."

"To your left," Shandra said. "See if you can sit on me like Kyla did."

"What'd you do? Sit in here with the lights off to trick Kyla?"

Shandra laughed. "You wouldn't want her to miss that part of blind camp, would you?"

"Well, I was going to tell you it's nice to see you again, but now I'm not so sure. Let's see whether Kyla survived first." Carmina turned to Kyla and shook her hand, "Welcome!"

Kyla felt warmth and confidence in Carmina's voice and handshake. "Okay, I'm confused," Kyla said. "How'd you know where I was if you didn't know where Shandra was? Do you see or not?"

"Not," Carmina said. "Blinded by a wild case of **juvenile diabetes**. Now who can tell Kyla how I knew where she was?"

"She was talking when we came in," Nadia said.

"Right!" Carmina said. "So what allows you to come to this exclusive camp?"

"Humpty-Dumpty eyes," Kyla replied.

"Okay, now *I'm* confused," Carmina said. "Never heard of Humpty-Dumpty eyes."

"Really bad myopia plus a basketball injury gave me a detached retina. Dr. Goodwin fixed the detachment, but all the king's horses and all the king's men couldn't give me back my vision again because I also have juvenile macular degeneration."

"Well, guess that qualifies you to be here," Carmina said. She reached out and hugged Kyla, then pressed a button on her watch. An electronic voice said, *Seven-ten P.M.* "Okay, gang, we've got twenty minutes to stash our gear and get ourselves to the rec building for our orientation meeting. Now let's give a high five for Cabin 3, sure to be the best!"

Orientation Night included the week's ground rules and team activities to help campers get to know each other. The cabins competed against each other in giant beach ball games and blindfold relays. Cabin 3's fiercest competition was with the senior high boys in Cabin 6. In the final parachute drill, the boys beat the girls by one second.

Carmina and her campers tramped back to their cabin singing sad, silly loser songs. Carmina took off Scout's harness and let the girls play with him for a few minutes. Once they were in bed, Shandra began a bell-ringer story where each person added to the story when they heard their assigned number of rings.

Carmina finished the night by leading them in more silly camp songs. Kyla drifted off to sleep listening to Carmina's voice.

The next day, Cabin 3 jogged around the lake before breakfast and practiced archery after breakfast. It took Kyla a few times to get the hang of pulling back on the bow while balancing the arrow on her finger, but she soon learned to enjoy the tension and zing that sent the arrow speeding toward the sound of the beeper located in the center of the target. When she made a bull's-eye in the final round, her team cheered loudly.

Horseback riding followed archery. Kyla helped Lauren and Nadia mount and center themselves in their saddles. After lunch, Kyla became a beeper so the elementary kids knew which way to shoot the basketball. Later, everyone went swimming. Shandra zoomed through the water, amazing Kyla with her power and speed. "No wonder Carmina called you a shark swimmer!" Kyla told her.

That evening, the senior high campers went boating on the lake. Brent and Jake took Kyla with them.

"Do you see at all?" Kyla asked them.

"I'm legally blind, but I can read and see some stuff in the distance. My eyes rove around real fast trying to focus and stuff's blurry because I have **nystagmus** and **albinism**," Jake said.

"I have pretty good central vision," Brent said. "I just don't have any **peripheral vision** because I have **retinitis pigmentosa**."

"Well then, we'll make a good team," Kyla said. "My central vision's bad, but I can see out the sides of my eyes."

They paddled around the lake for a long time, sharing stories and frustrations. As they headed back to shore, Jake asked, "Can you see the sunset?"

"Only to my right. It's an orange glow," Kyla said.

"No, it's not to the right," Brent countered. "I see it straight ahead." They all laughed and started singing, "Three blind mice, three blind mice . . ." as they tied up the rowboat.

On Thursday, the senior high campers went on an all-day nature trail hike. They left camp with walking sticks and backpacks filled with water, snacks, and box lunches. Their guide, Mr. Hunter, instructed them to feel the texture of the bark on trees, to finger the different leaves on plants and bushes, and to pick up pinecones, special rocks, and seed pods near the path. He challenged them to sniff out flowers and musty areas and to pay attention to moss, pine needles, and stones underfoot. He promised points to the first campers to identify streams or waterfalls by listening to the sound of the water.

"And remember, there are many Braille signs along the way that identify things," Mr. Hunter said.

Kyla walked with Carmina and Scout. Carmina shared some of her battles with a **volatile** case of juvenile diabetes. Losing her sight had been hard. She'd gone to a special school for the blind to learn how to take care of herself and gotten a guide dog so she could go to college.

"I don't know what I'd do without Scout," she said. "He helps me get around campus and even knows when my—"

Kyla grabbed Carmina as she slumped to the ground. "Mr. Hunter!" Kyla called, "Carmina fainted, and she's all clammy." Kyla shook Carmina, calling, "Carmina! Wake up, Carmina!"

Scout barked and pawed at Carmina's backpack. Kyla unzipped the backpack and found a pill bottle. Mr. Hunter read the label: "For diabetic emergency. Place one tablet under tongue."

Kyla popped the lid and removed a pill.

"It's a concentrated *glucose* pill that reverses a low *sugar level*," Mr. Hunter said. Within seconds after receiving the pill, Carmina began to stir.

"Carmina, are you okay?" Kyla asked, her heart hammering in her chest.

"Yes," Carmina answered slowly. "Thanks . . . to you."

"And to Scout," Kyla said.

The rest of camp rushed by. Kyla learned to laugh at herself when she ran into the volleyball net or overshot the basketball net. She fished, canoed, used paddleboats, and even tried rock climbing.

The final night featured a talent show and campfire. Cabin 3 trailed Cabin 6 by ten points. The girls spent hours preparing humorous skits dealing with the misconceptions sighted people have about blind people. Carmina sang a line of "Nobody Knows the Trouble I've Seen" to start each skit. Lauren, Nadia, Shandra, and Kyla made each one more tragic than the last. By the time they finished, all the campers were on their feet shouting, "More! More!"

Their performance earned them the Cabin-of-the-Year Award. The girls hoisted their trophy high and sang their way to the bonfire where campers talked about their week.

Kyla waited until the end to speak. "I didn't really want to come here—a camp for the blind—because I didn't think I was blind." She paused. "Well, I was more blind than I knew, because I just saw my own problems. Now I know I'm not alone and that people who have trouble seeing can still enjoy life. They just have to find different ways to see."

As Kyla walked back to her cabin, she saw the flicker of lightning bugs in the darkness around her. She smiled, thinking of her father, who ever since she was small had called her "Lightning Bug" because of her bright hair. Maybe, just maybe, she was a little like a firefly in other ways too. The tiny insects wouldn't shine so bright if the night weren't so dark.

She knew she would have plenty of dark times ahead. But her mind was made up. The darker it got, the brighter she would shine.

WHO USES WHITE CANES?

People with severe visual limitations who've decided they're tired of bumping into things and are determined to take charge of their lives, that's who!

Like learning to ski or swim, learning to use a white cane takes courage, determination, a sense of humor, and lots of time and patience.

Young people sometimes refuse to consider using a cane because they don't want to advertise their inability to see or to be "different." Getting over these hang-ups and the fears that accompany cane travel involves learning to search for solutions. The most important thing a student must bring to cane travel is the willingness to try. Mastering the skill leads to empowerment and a satisfying sense of independence.

Canes come in many different sizes and are made of wood, aluminum tubing, solid fiberglass, fiberglass tubing, and carbon fiber compound tubing. Each material has different characteristics of strength, weight, and flexibility.

Some canes can be folded when not in use.

WHAT'S INVOLVED IN HAVING A GUIDE DOG?

Those who are blind or legally blind may apply for a guide dog. The evaluation process is intensive. It usually takes about two to four weeks for your request to be accepted and another four to six weeks until you go for training. Those desiring a guide dog should:

- Be old enough to assume all responsibility for her care. Because of the special bond that's created, you, not your parents, must be the one who feeds, waters, grooms, cares for her health needs, provides a place for her to exercise and sleep, and cleans up after her. Sixteen seems to be about the right age to think about getting a dog.
- Be ready to acknowledge that you need a dog. If you still have usable vision, you will be safer if you help identify buildings and read signs and traffic lights, but you must be willing to trust your dog to do what he has been trained to do.
- Have good orientation skills using a white cane before working with a dog.
- Be willing to be different. Schools, colleges, and other public places are required to allow you to have a guide dog, but people will be curious. Many will want to pet your dog. You will have to explain that your dog is working as your eyes when he's in harness and must not be distracted.

Becky Barnes, from Guiding Eyes for the Blind, says, "Having a dog to help you at college is great. It's important to make arrangements ahead of time and to take a kennel, crate, or tether for securing the dog when off duty. At first, roommates and classmates will be curious and not sure what's expected. If you teach them to allow the dog to work for you when in harness but encourage them to play with the dog when out of harness, they'll soon view your dog as a valued member of the class."

YOU'RE NOT THE ONLY ONE
WHO GOES TO SCHOOL

Guide dogs undergo enough education to qualify them on a master's level!

The process begins with careful breeding. Once the puppies are able to leave their mother, they enter an elementary program where trained puppy raisers instill confidence while teaching specific obedience and socialization skills. The puppies are evaluated every three months.

If all goes well, they'll receive a "Guide Dog in Pre-Training" coat at about eight months, boosting the training to a secondary level.

A dog who is training to be a guide dog must learn to sit and stay.

These dogs are being trained at The Seeing Eye in Morristown, New Jersey.

After several more months, they'll be tested for entrance into a very vigorous training program, which can be likened to a college education. Because of the great responsibility they'll have in assisting the blind, guide dogs must demonstrate:

- intelligence
- a willingness to learn
- a good memory
- the ability to concentrate for long periods
- great attention to sound and touch
- excellent health

If they seem nervous, aggressive, or upset by cats or other dogs, they're released from the program.

Guide dogs allow blind people to move confidently on busy city sidewalks.

Those in the top half of their class are admitted to a rigorous guide dog training program where they will learn to:

- walk in a straight line to the left and just ahead of the handler
- respond to verbal and leash commands
- stop at curbs
- exercise selective disobedience for the safety of the handler
- take handlers around objects and get through narrow spaces safely
- stop for stairs
- ignore distractions
  (Adapted from "How Guide Dogs Work" by Tom Harris on howstuffworks.com)

About 72 percent of those who finish their "college education" will qualify to enter the master's level of study where they will be paired with their master. Great attention is given to selecting the right dog for the right person. Weeks of training and supervision help dog and master learn to work together.

By the time they graduate, both dog and master will have earned a master's degree in the art of understanding and trusting each other. Together, they'll make a Master Team for many years.

SPORTS, GAMES, AND RECREATION

Blindness and visual problems certainly make sports, games, and recreational activities more challenging. But they don't eliminate them.

Exercise, competition, and fun are just as important for those who have trouble seeing as for those with good vision. Visual disabilities usually require some adaptations in how games are played and may rule out a few activities for safety reasons.

Those who want to be active find ways to do it. Some do it for fun. Some train and compete at Olympic levels. Their drive, competitive spirit, and athletic prowess inspire and energize all who watch.

Some of the activities enjoyed by those with visual handicaps include:

- hiking
- rock climbing
- camping
- canoeing
- kayaking
- rafting
- sailing
- swimming
- water skiing
- ropes courses
- beep baseball
- horseback riding
- bowling
- judo
- track and field
- power lifting
- wrestling
- tandem cycling
- alpine skiing
- Nordic skiing
- snowshoeing
- ice-skating

(Adapted from American Council of the Blind, www.acb.org)

Board games can also be adapted for use by those who can't see. Checkers, chess, Scrabble, and many other games

This child, who is blind, enjoys learning to play catch.

Workers at Camp Abilities in New York State teach campers how to participate in a variety of sports.

can be purchased with special boards and playing pieces that allow the visually impaired to feel where the pieces are.

The American Council of the Blind has an extensive list of organizations that promote sports and recreational activities by providing helpful products or services.

OLYMPIC-LEVEL COMPETITION

The United States Association of Blind Athletes (USABA) organizes the following athletic competitions for those who are visually impaired or blind:

- judo
- swimming
- track and field
- alpine skiing
- Nordic skiing
- power lifting
- wrestling
- tandem cycling
- goalball

USABA athletes compete in summer and winter Paralympic games, held in Olympic facilities two weeks after the end of the regular Olympic games. Thousands of outstanding ath-

Campers at Camp Abilities enjoy going for a ride in a rowboat.

letes from around the world participate in the Paralympic games. Categories of competition are determined by the physical disabilities of the contestants.

Other opportunities include international events as well as competitions and camps at local, regional, and national levels.

To be eligible to compete in USABA programs, a person's:

- distance vision must be 20/200 or less. This means that what a normally sighted person can see at two hundred feet is not able to be seen by the person with visual impairment until it is twenty feet or closer.
- field of vision is twenty degrees or less. Field of vision refers to the area a person can see without moving

Because a person cannot see does not mean she cannot enjoy sports, including rowing.

Young people at Camp Abilities play goalball.

the eyes or head. A twenty-degree field of vision is like looking through a peephole in a door.

For further information, contact the USABA at USABA.org.

WHAT'S GOALBALL?

Goalball is a game where both sighted and sight-impaired players can compete on an equal basis. If anyone has an advantage, however, it's those who are blind. The reason? All players are blindfolded!

The game was invented in Austria following World War II to provide recreation for blind veterans. It is played on a floor about the size of a volleyball court. Lines with a cord under them are taped to the floor so players can feel where they are. Three players on each team try to roll a basketball-sized ball with a bell in it around the players on the opposite team so they can get it across the opponent's goal line.

Goalball can be used at camps and in gym classes to give young people an idea of what it's like to be blind. It is also played on an Olympic level. And there, the goal is to score goals with no excuses about how hard it is to be blind!

BLINDNESS IS JUST A SMALL PART OF WHO YOU ARE

Cara Dunne-Yates was blinded at age five by retinoblastoma, a rare cancer of the eyes. Her stepfather helped her fight back by teaching her to ski. They pioneered a method in which she followed him down the slopes.

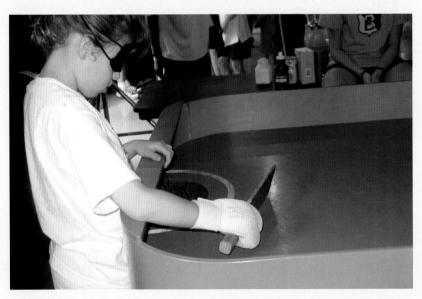

Special modifications allow youngsters who are blind to take part in a wide variety of sports and activities.

Blind does not mean unable! A student at the Batavia School for the Blind in New York State likes working with his hands.

Students who cannot see use their hands to learn and explore.

She soon began winning alpine skiing events and qualified for the World Championships as one of the youngest members of the United States Disabled Alpine Ski Team. Cara collected over ten Olympic and World Championship medals as she traveled throughout Europe, Canada, and the United States as a teen racer.

Cara put ski competitions on hold to study economics and Japanese at Harvard University. While a student, she lived in Japan, was elected president of her class, and graduated magna cum laude.

After graduation, Cara began skiing competitively again

and working with visually impaired children who wanted to ski. Forced to give up skiing to battle a deadly bone cancer of the face genetically related to the eye cancer she'd had as a child, Cara created a Braille menu business, wrote feature stories, entered UCLA's law school, and threw herself into a new sport: tandem bike racing.

Since 1994, Cara and racing partner Scott Evans have competed in numerous cycling championships around the world. They took bronze and silver at the 1996 Paralympic games in Atlanta, making Cara one of the few athletes to win medals in both winter and summer competitions.

Cara and Scott also won the European tandem champi-

Guide dogs help individuals who cannot see to live independent and self-sufficient lives.

onships in Holland in 1997. That same year, Cara became the first blind athlete to compete in a mainstream mountain bike race, placing second in an all-sighted field. She also graduated from law school with an emphasis on health policy and bioethics.

In 1998, Cara married Spencer Yates, a cycling teammate. Their daughter, Elise, was born in January 2000. After competing in the Paralympic games in Sydney, Australia later that year, Cara learned she would have to battle cancer a third time because a rare abdominal sarcoma had spread to her liver.

Cara puts her life into perspective by saying, "Blindness is no big deal. It's just a small part of who you are. Cancer, however, is life threatening. I have to deal with the possibility of dying and leaving my little girl every day. With blindness, the biggest challenge is other people's negative atti-

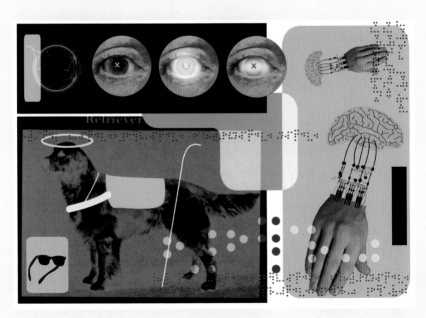

People who are blind use various tools and special adaptations to help them function in a seeing world.

tudes. It takes a little time to figure out how to do things differently but there really are no barriers."

Cara sees life as "a gift of grace, even when it's weird and unpredictable. My job is to teach people to reach out with both hands and scoop up life. Partly because it's the only life you have and it's good, and partly because there's no time to wait for things to get better or easier.

"Life doesn't stop spewing out problems. It doesn't slow down so you can tie your shoelaces. You can love life even as you are questioning its certainty and battling its harshest forces. Life isn't about being called a hero for doing something you love or for battling your way through disease. Life is all about the round-cheeked kiss of a cuddly toddler. It's all about the falling rain and the warmth of a loved husband's hand. It's all about finding joy in the darkest hours."

This Seeing Eye® dog helps her owner find joy and independence.

FURTHER READING

Alexander, Sally Hobart. *Mom Can't See Me.* New York: Macmillan Publishing Company, 1990.

Alexander, Sally Hobart. *Mom's Best Friend.* New York: Macmillan Publishing Company, 1992.

Alexander, Sally Hobart. *On My Own.* New York: Macmillan Publishing Company, 1994.

Alexander, Sally Hobart. *Taking Hold: My Journey into Blindness.* New York: MacMillan Publishing Company, 1994.

Alexander, Sally Hobart. *Do You Remember the Color Blue? And Other Questions Kids Ask About Blindness.* New York: Viking, 2000.

Gibson, William. *The Miracle Worker.* New York: Bantam Books, 1997.

Kess-Gardner, Jacqui. *The Incredible Journey . . . The Jermaine Gardner Story.* Baltimore, Incredible Journey Productions, 2002. Available by calling 866-303-JAZZ (5299).

Rodriquez, B. *Sarah's Sleepover.* New York: Viking Press, 2000.

Runyan, Marla, with Sally Jenkins. *No Finish Line, My Life as I See It.* New York: G. P. Putman's Sons, 2001.

Weihenmayer, Erik. *Touch the Top of the World, A Blind Man's Journey to Climb Farther than the Eye Can See.* New York: Dutton, 2001.

VIDEO

The Miracle Worker, Walt Disney Home Video.

FOR MORE INFORMATION

This is a partial list of the many organizations available to educate and assist those with visual impairments. Many provide links to other organizations. Be sure to check with your local school system, libraries, and state organizations for help in finding guidance and assistance in your area.

American Academy of Ophthalmology
655 Beach Street, P.O. Box 7424
San Francisco, CA 94109-7424
(415) 561-8500
www.aao.org

American Council of the Blind
1155 15th Street, NW, Suite 1004
Washington, DC 20005
(800) 424-8666
(202) 467-5081
www.acb.org

American Foundation for the Blind
11 Penn Plaza, Suite 300
New York, NY 1001
(800) AFBLIND (Toll Free Hotline)
(800) 232-3044 (Publications)
afbinfo@afb.net
afb.org

American Macular Degeneration Foundation
P.O. Box 515
Northampton, MA 01061-0515
413-268-7660
www.macular.org

American Optometric Association
243 Lindbergh Boulevard

St. Louis, MO 63141
(888) 396-EYES (3937)
(314) 991-4100
www.aoanet.org

American Printing House for the Blind, Inc.
1839 Frankfort Avenue
Louisville, KY 40206
(502) 895-2405
info@aph.org
www.aph.org

Association for Macular Diseases
210 East 64th Street
New York, NY 10021
(212) 605-3719
macular@macular.org
www.macular.org

Blind Children's Center
www.blindcntr.org

Braille Circulating Library
2700 Stuart Avenue
Richmond, VA 23220
(804) 359-3743

The Foundation Fighting Blindness
11435 Cronhill Drive
Owings Mills, MD 21117-2220
(888) 394-3937; (800) 683-5551 (TTY)
(410) 568-0150; (410) 363-7139 (TTY)
www.blindness.org

Guiding Eyes for the Blind
611 Granite Springs Road

Yorktown Heights, N.Y. 10598
(800) 942-0149

Leader Dogs for the Blind
1039 South Rochester Rd.
Rochester, MI 48307-3115
(248) 651-9011
www.leaderdog.org

Lighthouse International
111 East 59th St.
New York, NY 10022-1202
(800) 829-0500
(212) 821-9200
info@lighthouse.org
www.lighthouse.org

Lions International
300 22nd Street
Oakbrook, IL 60570
(630) 571-5466
www.lions.org

Macular Degeneration International
6700 North Oracle Road, Suite 505
Tucson, AZ 85704
(800) 393-7634
(520) 979-2525
www.maculardegeneration.org/

National Association for Visually Handicapped
www.navh.org

National Braille Press
www.nbp.org

National Eye Institute
National Eye Health Program
2020 Vision Place
Bethesda, MD 20892-3655
(301) 496-5248
www.nei.nih.gov

National Federation of the Blind
1800 Johnson Street
Baltimore, MD 21230
(410) 659-9314
nfb@nfb.org
www.nfb.org

National Information Center for Children and Youth with Disabilities
(NICHCY)
Box 1492
Washington, DC 20013-1492
(202) 884-8200
(800) 695-0285
(202) 884-8441
nichcy@aed.org
www.nichcy.org

National Resource Center for Blind Musicians
Director, David Goldstein
600 University Avenue
Bridgeport, CN 06601
(203) 366-3300
102730.163@compuserve.com

New York Institute for Special Education/Education of the Blind
(N.Y.I.S.E.)
999 Pelham Parkway
Bronx, NY 10469
(718) 519-7000, Ext. 315

Fax: (718) 231-9314
112213.2114@compuserve.com
www.nyise.org

Overbrook School for the Blind
6333 Malvern Ave.
Philadelphia, PA 19151-2597
(215) 877-0313
www.obs.org

Prevent Blindness America
500 E. Remington Road
Schaumburg, IL 60173
(800) 331-2020
infor@preventblindness.org
www.preventblindness.org

United States Association of Blind Athletes
33 North Institute Street
Colorado Springs, CO 80903
(719) 630-0422
usabab@usa.net
USABA.org

Vacation Camp for the Blind
111 Summit Park Rd.
Spring Valley, NY 10977
(212) 625-1616
www.visionsvcb.org

Publisher's Note:

The Web sites listed on these pages were active at the time of publication. The publisher is not responsible for Web sites that have changed their address or discontinued operation since the date of publication. The publisher will review and update the Web sites upon each reprint.

GLOSSARY

adaptive physical education classes: Physical education classes designed to allow those with physical disabilities to participate safely.

albinism: A group of inherited conditions in which the genes do not make the usual amount of pigment normally found in the eyes, skin, or hair.

Braille: A system of writing and reading using raised dots.

Braillewriter: A machine similar to a typewriter that imprints Braille letters on special paper.

chopper stork: An air ambulance.

closed-circuit TV: A video system used to supply text for spoken dialogue or to enlarge printed materials.

Coates Disease: An eye inflammation caused by a malformation of the blood vessels in the retina. Blood builds up behind the eye, causing scarring, and sometmes causes the retina to become detached. It usually affects only one eye, and it is most common in male children.

dystrophy: The degeneration of something.

embosser: A device that can be used to make a Braille printout from a computer.

glucose: Sugar.

guide dog: A dog that's been specially trained to assist those who are blind.

juvenile diabetes: A condition in which people are unable to properly use the glucose in their bloodstream because of a lack of insulin activity, so named because its onset is primarily during childhood.

juvenile macular degeneration: A condition in which the macula is not functioning properly in a young person.

macula: The small spot near the center of the retina that provides sharp, central vision.

macular degeneration: The gradual deterioration of the macula that leads to blurred central vision.

mobility instructor: Someone who assists those who are visually impaired or blind to learn to get around safely on their own.

myopia: Nearsightedness. The inability to focus clearly on things in the distance.

nystagmus: Rapid eye movements that may occur with a variety of visual problems.

optical aids: Items including a variety of specialized spectacles, telescopes, absorptive lenses, magnifiers, and adaptive devices that assist in seeing.

peripheral vision: Side vision.

refracts: Distorts by viewing through a medium such as glass.

residual vision: The vision that a person with visual loss is still able to use.

retinal detachment: Separation of the retina from the layer of blood vessels behind it that supply oxygen and nutrients to the eye.

retinitis pigmentosa: An inherited disorder that causes night blindness and tunnel vision.

Stargardt's: The most common form of inherited juvenile macular dystrophy.

stylus: A pointed instrument used to push dots through special heavy paper to write Braille. It is used with a hinged metal or plastic slate that serves as a guide under and on top of the paper. People can write Braille with a stylus and slate at about the same rate that others write with a pen or pencil.

sugar level: The glucose level in the bloodstream.

tactually: Relying on the sense of touch.

vitreous: The clear jelly that fills the eyeball outside the lens.

volatile: Characterized by a rapid or unexpected change.

INDEX

BIOGRAPHIES

Patricia Souder has written two biographies, a collection of drama sketches, and a variety of stories and articles for children and adults. She has also contributed to several gift books and created and directed numerous musical productions. She directs the Montrose Christian Writers' Conference and works part-time as a registered nurse.

Dr. Lisa Albers is a developmental behavioral pediatrician at Children's Hospital Boston and Harvard Medical School, where her responsibilities include outpatient pediatric teaching and patient care in the Developmental Medicine Center. She currently is Director of the Adoption Program, Director of Fellowships in Developmental and Behavioral Pediatrics, and collaborates in a consultation program for community health centers. She is also the school consultant for the Walker School, a residential school for children in the state foster care system.

Dr. Carolyn Bridgemohan is an instructor in pediatrics at Harvard Medical School and is a board-certified developmental behavioral pediatrician on staff in the Developmental Medicine Center at Children's Hospital, Boston. Her clinical practice includes children and youth with autism, hearing impairment, developmental language disorders, global delays, mental retardation, and attention and learning disorders. Dr. Bridgemohan is coeditor of *Bright Futures Case Studies for Primary Care Clinicians: Child Development and Behavior*, a curriculum used nationwide in pediatric residency training programs.

Cindy Croft is the State Special Needs Director in Minnesota, coordinating Project EXCEPTIONAL MN, through Concordia University. Project EXCEPTIONAL MN is a state project that supports the inclusion of children in community settings through training, on-site consultation, and professional development. She also teaches as adjunct faculty for Concordia University, St. Paul, Minnesota. She has worked in the special needs arena for the past fifteen years.

Dr. Laurie Glader is a developmental pediatrician at Children's Hospital in Boston where she directs the Cerebral Palsy Program and is a staff pediatrician with the Coordinated Care Services, a program designed to meet the needs of children with special health care needs. Dr. Glader also teaches regularly at Harvard Medical School. Her work with public agencies includes New England SERVE, an organization that builds connections between state health departments, health care organizations, community providers, and families. She is also the staff physician at the Cotting School, a school specializing in the education of children with a wide range of special health care needs.